D1474093

DREAM
SYMBOLOGY
DICTIONARY

Michael Schwartz

DREAM
SYMBOLOGY
DICTIONARY

Michael Schwartz

Dream Symbology Dictionary
by Michael Schwartz

Published by:
Inner Health Books
950 Sundance
New Braunfels TX 78130

©2011 Inner Health Books
Printed in the United States of America

Table of Contents

Preface

If you are reading this, it tells me that you are a seeker of deeper knowledge of the Self. Seeking is a worthy pursuit with great rewards for those who persevere and grow within from the knowledge gained. There are many ways of looking at anything. People see what they want to see, and hear what they want to hear, as well.

What is offered in this work is a perspective based on the Universal Teachings. The Teachings are based on the Fundamental Laws and Principles that are the foundation of how life works. These Laws and Principles are the Guiding Force in the Creation process. The Teachings are an expression of understanding within the Laws and Principles.

Introduction

Throughout this work I talk about the Universal Teachings as the fundamental principles on which all of this information is based. You hear Universal Teachings being spoken almost daily in your life, sometimes in clichés such as, "What goes around comes around," and, "You get what you give." In religious services you will hear things such as, "Ask and you shall receive," "Turn the other cheek," as well as "Resist not evil."

Here is an example of how it works: If you have ever been in an argument with someone, you may have experienced that the more you responded in that argument the more intense it became. Things are said that are often regretted later. However, if you walk away from the argument, that energy has nowhere to go and will dissipate. This is why it is good to "Turn the other cheek" and "Resist not evil."

There is another Teaching my wife and I personally like because it helps to keep everything in perspective, "First remove the plank from your own eye, and then you will see clearly to remove the speck from your brother's eye." This says: look at your own belief system and examine your perception of things before you start making judgments about another person. In your mind you are absolutely 100% right. In the other person's mind they are 100% right. "Right" is a relative term, meaning that everyone sees things from their own perspective. Everything is viewed and experienced through their personal belief system[1], as is yours.

Another Teaching along the same lines is, "Know what is before your eyes and all the mysteries will be revealed." This implies that if you know what you are looking at you are seeing your concepts in action, considering that everything that is around you is of your co-creation. You are co-creating your reality based on your subconscious expectations. Your partner in this ongoing creation is the Creative Continuum called God.

A POINT OF VIEW

The mind is the operator of an electromagnetic generator known as the brain. As such, it is constantly sending out electromagnetic waves. It is attracting or repelling positively charged atoms or ions. These particles form molecules. The form of molecules could be in the form of a person or a thing. Consequently, you are co-creating the events in your life, as well as drawing people to you. In the same regard, you are repelling things away from you.

Look at how a magnet works. The positive attracts the negative, the negative attracts the positive. The positive repels positive, the negative repels the negative. Your "magnetic mind" is doing the exact same thing, drawing things and people to you and repelling others, as well. This is based on your need to fulfill subconscious expectations.

This is talked about In the Universal Teaching, "Ask and ye shall receive," because the asking is being done at a subconscious level. If you do not know what you are asking you will not be able to control the results. Look at your life and everything that is going on around you because it is a representation, a manifestation of the energies at work within you.

Universal Teachings

The reason the Teachings are called Universal is because, regardless of religious convictions or spiritual inclination, these truths are applicable to your situation and life.

The Teaching of "Cast your bread upon the water" is equal to "You get back what you give out" and "What goes around comes around." If you give out good energy, love, tolerance and acceptance that is what you will get back from people. When you do not, it is because there is something else that you need to hear, see, feel or experience. So, you create a different expressive energy to attract what you need. What you get back from people is the fulfillment of subconscious expectations. What are they? Do you know which subconscious concepts motivate you?

The Teachings provide an insight into the human mind. The unique metaphysical[2] perspective gleaned from them allows for clarity of the energies involved in every transaction you take part in. The Universal Teachings are steps for insightful growth and Self-development.

From long years of experience, I feel assured that the perspective offered will be of value on multiple levels.

How to Use This Information

As an individual seeking Self-knowledge on all levels, the application of this work will assist you in gaining a deeper understanding of why and who you are. All events and situations are created by you under the direction of your subconscious concepts. Thus, the event/situation will manifest according to those directives. One such set of circumstances and events may become an illness. These are the result of conflict between the Inner Self and the Outer Self; Inner Self, in this case, being the Spiritual Self, and the Outer Self being the ego.

You often have desires of what you would like to do, yet at subconscious levels you do not feel you have the right, the authority, or the power to do them. Therefore, there is conflict. The conflict will ultimately manifest as discomfort or disease.

The information contained within this work will provide you with all types of different insights that can lead to greater understandings. When you examine concepts, patterns of behavior and cycles, you can begin to understand what is going on in your life and why things are the way they are. Learning to work with symbols in general, learning the methods and techniques for discerning what they are and analyzing them will allow you to gain even greater control over the energy of your life.

The statement that insights lead to understandings can be realized. It is the understandings that will ultimately lead to gaining control over patterns of behavior. When one has control over patterns of behavior, one is truly on a path of mastery.

By studying and learning symbology you can expand your understanding of life in general.

How Life Works

Living is complex. Living your life is a matter of fulfilling subconscious expectations. It is what all people live for.

The reason for this, the drive, the determination and the motivation for fulfilling your subconscious expectations is based on your need for acceptance. Acceptance is sought from the mother. She was the doorway into the Material Plane.

You are a spiritual being encased in a material body/vehicle. You, as well as every person, want to return to the peace and tranquility of the Spiritual Plane. Because of that deep subconscious drive, no one wants to be cut off from the doorway home. No one wants to be rejected. All children want and seek their mother's approval.

You want to be what she expects you to be.

There are two avenues that you could have taken to fulfill these expectations and maintain approval. The "goody two shoes" is going to follow the orientation of their gender as demonstrated by the concepts of mom. Being just like mom is one form of acceptance. Dad represents mom's concept of a male. Everything that mom believes and expects a man to be can be found in "dad," and usually the female will marry someone with the same or similar male concepts that mom holds to be true.

It is through this parent-child relationship that concepts are presented and passed along. These concepts become the foundations for generating the expectations of what each individual believes they should be. Then people live their lives seeking to fulfill them, thus validating who they think they should be.

REJECTION AS A FORM OF APPROVAL

It is often very difficult to see rejection as a form of approval and acceptance. When you think about seeking acceptance from others you think about doing everything that is proper, right, socially acceptable and politically correct. Acceptance has many different ways and forms of manifesting. It all depends on the circumstances.

Rejection becomes a form of acceptance for some individuals. The reason for these energies, forces, and attitudes of rejection becoming the foundations of the patterns of behavior begins at the first awareness of conception. What is meant by "awareness of conception" is the moment that the woman in the relationship becomes aware of the fact that she is pregnant.

If this pregnancy is unplanned or unwanted for any number of reasons, it raises issues for every individual. There is a very subtle energy, maybe even a conscious energy that is created through the thought of, "I really do not want this to happen." However, because of religious and moral obligations the individual may feel they need to adhere to, the more likely it is that they will go through with the pregnancy. During this pregnancy, rejection will manifest in different ways on different levels. One example would surround events at the time of delivery, such as a long and difficult labor, the need for surgery and/or the child immediately becoming ill.

Rejection may also become more pronounced as energy at work when spirit enters into the fetus. This occurs around three months in uteri. This is when the fetus begins to move about. Once that begins to happen you are looking at additional feelings of rejection.

Now the individual knows that there is no turning back. This is real and this pregnancy is going to happen, and life is going to be changed forever. If there are elements of resentment, not wanting this to take place and resenting the fact that it is taking place, rejection energy is stimulated.

You are here to participate in the harmonizing of mankind with nature. This begins with harmonizing within oneself.

Life is a continual cleansing process. Misconceptions that you live by (man-made ideals, values, standards) require cleansing. By doing so, the Inner Self[3] can once again learn, express, and manifest the benefits and gifts that lie deep within the Inner/Spiritual Self. By incorporating the Universal Teachings into your daily awareness, insights are achieved that lead to greater understandings. Understandings lead to control. Control leads to Mastery.

UNDERSTANDINGS

In life you often hear and use the word understanding. You say you understand this or that. You rarely think of the definition of the word "understand," so here are a few to work with: Comprehension- the faculty by which one understands; intelligence. As an adjective: characterized by or having comprehension, good sense, or discernment. Compassionate; sympathetic. As a noun: it is the ability to learn, judge, or make decisions.

Based on this, you could say that there are things you truly know and understand and there things you do not. When it comes to the Self, you may only think you know or understand.

Even within the concept of understanding there are very distinct levels. For instance, there are basic understandings that affect life. A prime example is the understanding that you require food and water in order to exist. Understandings are essential to successful living on all levels: emotional, social, physical/material and, especially, spiritual. Developing the depth of your own understandings and discovering new ones will lead to mastery of your life in greater degrees than you are experiencing right now.

There is another level of understanding: the fundamental understanding. A perfect example is: everything material and gaseous in the universe is made up of atoms. Atoms have a positive or negative charged electromagnetic energy. Through the process of aggregation, atoms bond together to create molecules and they, in turn, accumulate to become something else. A cell or a piece of furniture, the combinations are countless.

Another amazing fundamental understanding is that the brain is an electromagnetic generator. Most people are unaware of this understanding. This is an incredible piece of information to help develop a better understanding of how you are co-creating your reality and how the Teaching of "Ask and you shall receive" works. The catch is that you must be in control of your subconscious desires in order to have true control over your manifestations.

When you take both understandings and work them together, you can see that your personal reality is a result of you electromagnetically drawing those "atoms/molecules" to you that manifest as a person, a place and/or a thing that you are facing and experiencing. On the same note, you are repelling that energy away from you. The questions arise, "What am I attracting to me?" and "What am I keeping away from me?"

I choose the words "keeping away" because they imply more than repelling. There are some energy manifestations that you want in your life but do not have. One such example might be having extra spending money. Through the process of understanding, you can attract to you or "keep away" specific energies. The mechanism that runs the electromagnetic bio-generator is the mind. The mind is influenced by concepts. Concepts affect the flow of the magnetic energy.

CONCEPTS, PATTERNS AND CYCLES

The following section of the material explains the basic workings of the mind. It discusses the principles of how personal belief systems are built and why people strive to sustain and maintain them. The basics that you will deal with are concepts (ideas you hold to be true and live by), patterns (repetitive acts of behavior based upon those concepts), and cycles (the basic movement of life).

Concepts, behavioral patterns, and cycles are interrelated. Concepts are the foundation of patterns. Personal behavioral patterns flow in cycles. Concepts are simply the ideals, standards, values and guides that you hold to be true. These concepts mold the way you think and feel about yourself, other people, and the world. Thus, your actions and reactions are stimulated and governed by your concepts.

Each idea or concept that you maintain about yourself becomes part of the foundation stones of your belief system. Upon this foundation, each idea or concept becomes part of the whole. You build your belief system on what you expect and accept to be true or real. From your belief system (concepts), you form behavioral patterns about how to act in the many different situations in life. How you manifest and act in each aspect of your "Self" is influenced accordingly.

There are four aspects of the Self. The Physical/Material Self is the direct result of your thoughts; i.e., being thin, heavy, sickly, healthy, rich or poor. The Social Self may be one of an outgoing, gregarious kind of a person, or it may be a withdrawn or introverted kind of person. The Emotional Self may be quick to anger or intolerant or be loving, accepting and filled with patience. The Spiritual Self may be that of complete obedience to religious dogma and its work, or it may be agnostic, atheistic, or a seeker of Spiritual Truths.

Concepts are the root cause of all disharmonies. It is often a conflict of what the Self thinks it should be/do and what it really wants to be/do. The conflict can show itself in emotional outbreaks, violent actions, failure to complete, and many other destructive forms of behavior. Your concepts, when in conflict, will often lead to diseases.

The way you think and feel about yourself is the direct result of your concepts. Your self-image is a result of those concepts. You use your concepts to form your foundations and to construct your belief system. Your concepts influence how you feel about relationships with the opposite sex, as well as with your own sex. They influence your feelings toward your possessions, acquisitions, and food. In fact, your concepts influence and determine your feelings, thoughts, attitudes, likes and dislikes in every single area of your life. What you hold to be of value, what you feel to be true, what you are willing to accept, and not willing to accept are the results of your belief system.

Your belief system shades your perception, which is your point of view for everything in your life. It determines your belief in yourself and the things you think you can or cannot accomplish. For instance, if you were told as a child that you were sloppy and messy and could never do anything neatly, then you accepted those suggestions as true. They became a concept. You made it into an aspect of your self-image. Now, you continue to bring it into reality to validate the truth of it. Today, you are still sloppy, and messy and do not do anything neatly. This may manifest as disorganization, poor office keeping, wearing wrinkled clothes, messy hair, and the like.

If you were told that you would never be anything, then that suggestion may bear the fruit of incompleteness. By that, I mean that you may start a hundred projects, but never finish one because the completion would equal being "something," and this would go against the concept you have about yourself. You may have been told that you were selfish or bratty. Today, you are an individual who is overly concerned with yourself, and you can get very upset when things do not go your way.

These concepts are suggestions given and demonstrated to you. The concepts are not true reflections of the Inner Self. However, you have accepted those ideas and suggestions as true. You have lived seeing and hearing them uttered, demonstrated, inferred or insinuated by your parents.

Parents are your guides, not to impose, but to point the way toward reunification with The Creative Continuum, God. Each parent was once a child. It is through this parent-child relationship that concepts are passed from generation to generation[4,5]. You accept your parents concepts as the "way to be" because you do not want to be rejected. So, you accept their concepts, ideas, attitudes, feelings, likes and dislikes as your own. In this way, you have their approval, and a guarantee that they will not reject you. This is why, if your parents say or imply through actions, deeds, or thoughts that you are stupid, then you will accept that image as true. After all, they love you and you do not want to be rejected.

No One Wants To Be Rejected

Yet, there are those children and adults who always seem to seek rejection. In everything they do, in every relationship, project, and endeavor they seek rejection or failure. Why? Rejection is the form of approval these people have been taught. It satisfies their needs. You and everyone else accept the concepts presented. You incorporated them into your life and built your belief system and image around them. All this centered on your mode of approval.

For instance, if mom felt or thought that women are strong, sure, independent, authoritative, and dominant, and that men are weak, non-supportive, and non-authoritative, then the children will take these concepts and use them in the mode of approval that they have fashioned for themselves. Goody two shoes or rejection.

If the daughter in this relationship works under the concept of acceptance for approval, then she will be very much like mom and view men in the same way mom does. If, on the other hand, her form of approval is rejection, then she will be the opposite of mom and view men in the opposite perspective.

If the son in this relationship is working on acceptance for approval, he will be like his father because this is the accepted image of men. Yet, if he is seeking rejection for approval, then he obviously will be the opposite of his father. Now, you can take this example and interchange the concepts, where the daughter is like the father and the son like the mother, of the parents and children and find which mode you fit into.

Concepts are the root cause of all disharmonies, and disharmony will eventually lead to disease. Disharmony on a physical level is created when there is a mental conflict. This conflict exists between the Inner Spiritual Self and the Emotional Outer Self. The Inner seeks to do or be a certain way. The Outer does not believe it has the right, the ability or the authority to do or be it. Therein lies the conflict. Stated another way, conflict arises when the Outer Self is in disagreement with the Inner Self.

Dreams

A VEHICLE OF GUIDANCE AND DISCOVERY

Dreams, visions and conscious awareness are guides to help you gain greater clarity and awareness of where you are in a pattern of behavior at any time, thus allowing you the opportunity to change it. Everything you view or experience is a symbolic manifestation of a very specific concept and pattern of behavior expressed through thought. Remember, you are co-creating your reality with God, within and without.

When you understand the essence, the symbolic communication of what you are looking at, it puts you in a position of strength to deal with whatever is going on at that moment. Dreams and visions are precognitive because they are tied into the understanding that life flows in cycles[6]. Patterns of behavior flow in cyclical fashion and symbols tell you where you are in the cycle. By understanding that, it gives you an opportunity to change an attitude in order to change an outcome, and the pattern of behavior can manifest differently than it ever has before. This could help to put you into a cycle spiraling upwards versus a cycle that continues to roll along horizontally, forever cementing the cliché that history repeats itself.

Dreams are great tools because they give you a preview of the upcoming cycle or the upcoming day. Where you are, what energies are afoot, and what is going on. It takes you to the old cliché of "Forewarned is forearmed." By maintaining your awareness, what I will call a "matter-ological awareness,", it puts you in a position of strength and helps you see what could potentially be unfolding.

Remember that life is a matter of probabilities, possibilities and potentialities. Probability is the normal outcome of your patterns of behavior. It always has been and always will be because you do not catch on to it, you do not get it, and you cannot change it. There are possibilities where, if you have this or that under control, you would be able to manifest a different kind of energy with a different kind of understanding and, consequently, a different result/outcome or manifestation. Then you have potentialities. These are based on what you could achieve or change based on the degree and level of your understandings combined with emotional control. And so, you have probabilities, possibilities and potentialities.

WAKING THE DREAMING MECHANISM

When you have a hard time remembering your dreams, create a triggering device that will help you to recall your dreams. One easy technique is to tell yourself as you are falling asleep, "Mind, mind remember my dreams when I brush my teeth." This is an example of one of the many things that you can use as a trigger.

It is best to use something that you do everyday upon waking or shortly thereafter. The very best is to have a trigger that will help you remember while you are still lying in bed. It will also be helpful to keep a pad and pen by your bed so that as you remember you can write it down. In that way even the smallest detail will not be lost.

LUCID DREAMING

The concept of lucid dreaming[7] is first mentioned in a letter written by St. Augustine of Hippo in 415 A.D.[8] Basically it implies that you are awake at the same time that you are dreaming and, therefore, have a great degree of control within the dream.

On one level this sounds like a great plan and it is for co-creating the reality that you desire. On the other hand it alters the guidance that you could/would receive from your subconscious mind. And that is the most important aspect of dreaming because it prepares you to deal with the upcoming forces in days ahead.

VISIONS

There are different kinds of visions. There are hallucinations where you think you saw something but it was not there. There are directed visions where you were in meditation and were questioning your mind for an answer or insight to something and you saw something. You could also feel, smell, taste or hear something. Each of those would have to be viewed symbolically, as well. It is easier, and certainly the purposes of this book, to deal with that which you have eyes to see.

Hallucinations could very well be another form of communication. After all, you saw it and it might have some value for you if you question it, as opposed to dismissing it. Then there are mirages. Perhaps these are wishful thinking or the mind trying to create a reality; however, the individual does not have the personal power to alter matter enough to achieve what they desire. Since everything is energy and is made up of atoms, and since man has dominion over everything, if your mind were strong enough, clear enough, or free enough to allow the God within to manifest, you could turn sand into water.

There is so much written about dreams that you do not know what is right and what is not. What I would say to you about this work is that it is rooted in the Universal Teachings and they never fail to provide insights that can lead to understandings. Whether or not you achieve the understandings is up to you, because achieving an understanding requires questioning, pondering, analyzing and admitting to yourself that something is amiss, which is difficult for some to acknowledge. It is much easier for people to see everything in someone else than it is to see anything within themselves.

Dreams are both retro and pre-cognitive. Whenever you are in a situation and a concept is triggered by something someone said or did, your mind will respond to that stimuli based on past responses to similar energies. Your mind will draw on past experiences using the language of symbols. These symbols are the association you made with experiences you had, an object, smell, feeling or a sense of touch to create your symbol.

In dreams you "look back in order to see ahead;" a Universal Teaching; and will project your past reactions to given stimuli into the future so you can see what energy is at work in the upcoming cycle. By being forewarned you can be forearmed and you can make the necessary changes to avoid whatever it is the pre-cognitive symbol told you, which will flash back to a particular pattern of behavior.

Different Types of Dreams

NIGHTMARES

This is a situation where the information has been suppressed and the dream mechanism has not been utilized and has become rusty; a nightmare is the vehicle used in order to grab your attention. This is something that requires immediate thought, analysis, questioning, seeking, and awareness of what is going on in order to avoid problems and difficulties. Look around and question "What is going on? Why am I having these experiences? What is scaring me and why?"

FALLING

Falling in dreams could indicate that you have nothing to stand on and nothing to support you, that you are isolated and alone. What are you involved in that isolates you without external support that you feel you need? Keep in mind that you are never placed in a situation you cannot master.

DROWNING

This represents being overwhelmed by life, the material plane. Something is going on that you feel overwhelmed and unable to deal with from a position of strength. You are drowning in doubt and fear. Of course, there is always the PEA[9] that you have about being in deep water, water where you cannot stand and touch bottom. There is also the possibility that you are in a turbulent situation in which you feel adrift and overwhelmed.

RUNNING

You are running away or trying to get away from something that you feel may be hunting or attacking you. It could also represent that you are running away from responsibility. Look around and question what is going on that has you fleeing the scene.

Of course, there is the possibility that you are running after something. What is it that you are chasing? Why are you running after it? What do you think it will provide you?

❧

More often than not, you will find that symbols will provide guidance to you about what you are anticipating based on the particular pattern of behavior that you are operating with. Remember that whatever the pattern is, it has a forgone conclusion unless you change it, and the only way to change it is by seeing where you are in the cycle and acting appropriately by changing an attitude or initiating an action. That is what symbols tell you. That is how they guide you.

Again, this is an issue that requires your personal emotional association to discover its symbology as it applies to you and your situation. As with all symbols, you have to stretch your mind, which is the beauty of reading symbols because when you see how the guidance is working for you and how you can make it work for you, it helps to increase your depth of knowledge and understanding.

When symbols occur it is your mind's way of trying to wake you up to pay attention to something.

Looking back is part of a Universal Teaching. Looking back serves two purposes. You look back in order to see ahead, and you also look back to draw on past strengths and successes.

In dreams you can smell and taste things, because although you are in another reality, it is still something energetically that you can bring back with you in order to help you understand. It depends how your mind communicates with you.

You could have associations with different levels of interpretation. In all matters it always comes back to your PEA.

You can see by this that each symbol has multiple definitions. The real key to understanding is to relate it to what you are going through at the moment, and what you have gone through in the past that this particular symbol has meaning to you.

Building a Personal Symbol Dictionary

Symbols are messages from your subconscious mind to your conscious mind. They are a constant source of guidance. Whenever an animal is part of your dream, or if you realize that you are paying attention to a particular animal, then it is your mind telling you, "Here is a symbol, look at it, understand it so that you can make the appropriate decision." The decisions you make will lead you on the path that you want to travel. So, ideally, you will want to learn all you can about the animal that your attention has been drawn to. Understand what it means to you. Always seek to understand the furthest reaching definitions so that you do not overlook any possibilities for interpretations.

There are many symbol dictionaries currently in the marketplace. Each is the opinion, reflection, level of understanding and interpretation of the individual that writes it. There is no way to know how the interpretations are arrived at and on whose/what work they are based.

There are many different ways of interpreting symbols. The only way to bring insights and guidance is by bringing the symbol back to the Self. Symbols can be interpreted on a universal level. This means that everyone who sees it would interpret it the same, giving equal meaning to it. Perfect examples of these types of symbols are mathematic and road signs.

When you see a plus (+) sign you know to "add things up;" when you see the minus (–) sign you know to take something away from the sum. Road signs do the same by shape and color.

Red equals STOP; Green equals GO. Some signs tell you curve ahead, soft shoulder or steep grade ahead.

Your personal symbols do the very same thing. They are a very personal set of guides that assist you in mastery of your life, step by step.

THE PHYSICAL BOOK

You will want to divide your personal symbol book into four sections. Each section represents one aspect of your Self. The four selves are: Spiritual, Emotional, Physical/Material and Social.

Using a 3-ring binder would be best so you can insert pages. As your understanding of symbols grows and your depth of knowledge deepens, you are going to continually update and upgrade your personal symbol dictionary. There should also be a section for other symbols that have not been covered at the time of publication.

Your ability to identify symbols will become easier with practice. As you become aware of each symbol and the concept that it represents to you, you can place that symbol in the appropriate Self that is affected most. In most instances, the emotional Self is going to be the most fruitful ground because it directly relates to your concepts and belief system.

The symbology of one's life is manifested beginning with entry into the material plane (fetal stage) and continues through development through birth and so on. By the time an individual is three years old, the concepts that need to be understood, controlled and mastered will have been presented, accepted and incorporated into his/her being.

All issues, challenges, opportunities for mastery will be stimulated from your Emotional and Spiritual Self.

The circumstances surrounding the birth are also highly indicative of possibly the main issue that is to be resolved in this life cycle. Of course there are other things that play into a central theme and all of these become known as time unfolds.

By the time of being three years old, the concepts are fairly well established and the rest of life is directed toward creating the manifestations necessary for fulfilling and validating those concepts, those energetic realities.

I say energetic realities because, when it comes down to the nuts and bolts of material/physical reality, it is electromagnetically-based, in the sense that everything in our physical world is comprised of atoms, and atoms have spaces between their nucleus and outer rings, and are the manifestation of energy because they are constantly in motion. What appears to be solid is, in reality, something that is vibrating because it is in motion and has many open spaces. Now, what is it that creates physical reality? It is the attraction of one atom to others forming molecules. Molecules, having atoms, may also have a positive or negative charge. When molecules band together they create everything.

What is even more enlightening and interesting is the fact that the human mind is an electromagnetic generator. What that means is that you are constantly sending out a magnetic wave to attract or repel atoms, molecules, things, to you and away from you. By looking at everything that surrounds you and everything that you are involved in, it gives you an indication of the electromagnetic waves you are emitting. The direction or the support of those emissions is the subconscious concepts you maintain. They literally feed, guide, and run the generator that creates the magnetic wave. Through its directives, it is either attracting or repelling anything and everything to or from you[10]. What you have is what you created.

Reading Symbols

How to Interpret Symbols

We know that symbols are a form of guidance; a form of communication. Symbols are the hidden language of the mind. Now, you must extract that guidance from the message. How do you go about doing this? The first step, until it becomes a matter of automatic thought, is to write it down. This is very important, especially when it comes to dreams.

In working with your dreams or daily experiences, the first thing you must do is write down the entire experience. Write down every bit of it that you can remember. Read through it and underline all the obvious and important symbols. Next, write down the individual symbols and begin the interpretation process. After that is finished, reconstruct the "message" according to the interpretations. The following is an example of the process:

Step 1
I was driving in my car on the way to work when a dog jumped out in front of the car.

Step 2
I was driving in my car on the way to work when a dog jumped out in front of my car.

Step 3
I = myself
driving = operating my expression
car (type) = expression (solid, stable)
work = communicating, dealing with people

dog = companionship, of a temporary nature
jumped = uncontrolled move, unable to sustain for long
in front = ahead of me, the future
car = expression

Step 4
In expressing myself while working with people today, there will be feelings of a need for companionship. This may cause me to make some kind of uncontrolled move relating to the future, thus it may affect my communications with others.

Now that you have gone through the dream, experience or vision, you are ready to work with the energies of the day. You now know what Concepts and attitudes will be at work in your life, affecting your perception, understandings and your ability to evaluate correctly. Also, ask yourself what are the emotional overtones of the dream. Those will be the dominant emotions you will be dealing with in communicating with others and in expressing yourself. "Know what is in thy sight, and what is hidden from thee will be revealed to thee. For there is nothing hidden which will not manifest;" Gospel according to Thomas pg. 5, 10-14.

One thing that is very important in achieving your personal goals is creating your own "personal symbol" dictionary. The reason for this is because your mind makes emotional associations with pictures and things. This is done in order to communicate with you from the Guiding God Force within to your conscious awareness. In that way you can make the necessary adjustments on your path toward success and mastery on a very narrow path[11].

Remember that concepts stimulate you into performing in a particular way to achieve a particular result. The result is always designed to fulfill a subconscious expectation that you maintain about yourself. The fulfillment proves that it is true, even when it is not.

The concept uses developed patterns of behavior to achieve its desired result because it knows the pattern will always complete in the same way. Those patterns flow in cycles. The identifying and reading of symbols tells you where in the cyclical flow of the pattern you are. This allows you the opportunity to alter the pattern and change the outcome.

The following pages contain some basic common symbols with a universal interpretation. What the universal interpretation means for a symbol may be completely different from what it may mean for you personally. That is because every symbol in your life has a Personal Emotional Association. This means that as every event/situation/feeling/etc. has occurred in your life, you have associated it with some material/sound/ smell that was a part of it. You did not make the association with words, even though they were used.

Words are used to communicate the concepts and feelings that you have stored in your mind. The method for storage is an object/picture, sound, smell, taste or feeling. That is why all symbols will be one of those elements.

Dictionary

A

Accordion

This instrument is for personal expression[12]; something to make music/harmony, either alone or in a group. One would have to seek the Personal Emotional Attachment (PEA)[13] to truly know the significance of this symbol to you in relationship to what you are going through at the time.

Adrenal

The adrenal glands are the stress centers of the body. They secrete hormones that control key functions of the body, such as the making of carbohydrates and proteins, the working of the heart and lung systems, and the functioning of the muscles, kidneys and other organs. The adrenals also regulate blood sugar levels, thus, they affect energy levels as well.

Symbolically, malfunctions indicate doubt that would relate to areas of self-acceptance, ability to handle a situation, tolerance and the ability to grow within a situation. People are operating from a position of weakness if this gland is not working properly.

Air

Air is essential for life. It is a mixture of gases, one of which is oxygen. Oxygen is symbolic of Spirit/God because this is where God dwells, in the heavens, in the air.

Airboats

These represent a vehicle of expression. All vehicles that take you from point A to B are considered symbols of vehicles of personal expression.

In this case you are traversing the material plane symbolized by water. You are skimming over it and not necessarily involved in it (submerged in the sense that the hull of the boat does not go deep into the water). See also Vehicles of Expression.

In what ways are you floating by, not participating? Is it an escape vehicle? Is this something that you use to earn a living? Was it part of a vacation and left a lasting memory?

Air conditioning

If the air conditioner fails to operate it is comparable to the water pump on a car failing. The Symbologies are similar. Both are used for cooling down and when they malfunction it may be an indication of an upcoming overheated situation.

The situation would create a tendency towards an expression of anger, the heat building beyond capacity and exploding.

You need to question what is brewing; something is making you and the situations you are involved in become overheated, anxious, and angry.

Airplane

This is another vehicle of expression. It may be one mode of transportation that is particular to your expression, or an opportunity to escape from your responsibilities.

As a passenger, you are at the will of the pilot. You are subject to the concepts of whoever is in the pilot's seat from one point of view. As the passenger, you have given up your authority to be in control. How does that play with the rest of the symbols in the dream?

See also Vehicles of Expression.

Amethyst

This gem, like others, requires an in-depth study to understand its symbology. All gems and such may be gifts or losses and the correct interpretation will depend on your PEA to the gem.

Animals

All animals are symbolic of specific thoughts. The beauty of animals is that they are here to teach man different things about life and when you can see clearly, yourself. Each animal and insect has a very specific symbology. You can learn these through observation and also by understanding how they function as a species.

The other aspect to the symbology of an animal is the same fundamental principle that applies to every symbol: your PEA. This is the most important definition of a symbol and the one that should be used when seeking to understand a message.

Animals have very particular relationships with people. You need to look at the animal in question and the person to understand the relationship and its emotional symbology. It is always good to seek to understand the universal symbology, as this could present a perspective that leads to insight or understanding.

What an animal represents to you on a personal level is the only thing that really has any importance. Just to understand the symbology of an animal from a universal perspective is fine for your symbol dictionary, but you really need to know the ones that relate to you personally. All symbols are a way that God who dwells within uses to communicate with you, to keep you on that narrow path[14] that leads to light and life.

Another symbolic aspect of the animal kingdom is birthing; the first thing that takes place, the umbilical cord is severed. This tells you that, at a place in time, every person needs to cut the emotionally connected umbilical cord to his or her parents. After the animal is suckled and reaches the age of self-sufficiency after the parents have taught it to hunt and provide for itself, then the parent says, "Get out of my territory. This is my hunting ground. This is my domain. Get your own. It is a big world."

Ankle

The ankles and knees demonstrate the ability to be flexible in your direction and aspiration.

In relationship to your elbows and wrists, the flexibility is in how you handle situations and self-expression. They are also tied into standing and balance.

Antenna

Receptivity, your ability to receive input from within and externally, as well. The more you can tune into a clear signal the more knowledge you will accumulate.

The goal is to be very clear about what you are receiving and its affect upon you. Every day you are receiving stimuli. The question is, how does/did what you are receiving affect you? What concepts have been triggered and which pattern of behavior has been activated? Focus your antenna inward for the best results. Question everything you hear externally.

Keep in mind that you are looking and seeing, aspects of your antenna system, with vision that is shaded by your belief system and your emotions. The Universal Teaching that reflects this is, "And why beholdest thou the mote that is in thy brother's eye, but perceivest not the beam that is in thine own eye?" (KJV Luke 6:41)

Antiques

Old possessions may have a particular PEA for you, such as a hand-me-down from your grandparents or a family heirloom. They could also represent thoughts, inklings. In order to have a clear understanding of this type of communication you must view each piece of antique furniture, or whatever the object may be, from your past association with it.

Ants

Ants, from one perspective, are phenomenal because they are great community workers. They each serve a very specific function in their community. They are well-disciplined, very organized and task oriented. The community consists of the queen, the workers, defenders, feeders and nursery staff.

You may see them from another perspective, because if you have ants in the house, the first thing you want to do is kill them because they are there. It is not that they are dirty, but they will end up "cleaning out" the place. If you have crumbs lying around, they are going to go gather them. Once the food is gone, they are gone, too.

There are ants that bite and leave a burning sensation in the skin; these are prevalent throughout the southwest. They are called Fire ants. In this case you have a symbol of aggression, as well as petty annoyances.

If you have ants in your house, the next part of the symbology is to analyze the room they are in. Every room has its own unique symbolic interpretation.

Apple

Sustenance, Knowledge; all liquids and food materials are forms of sustenance. In this case there is the story from the Bible of the apple representing knowledge. This could apply to you, as well. However, there may be a more personal interpretation. An example may be that you were forced to eat apples. In that scenario the apple would represent imposition. As a teacher, the apple could be a symbol of appreciation. Think about all the ways that apples may figure in your life.

Appliances

The thing about appliances is that they will eventually break down and go bad. On one level of thinking, you would have the tendency to attribute any malfunction as just being normal life cycle usage and that thought would be absolutely correct. However, the other side of the coin is that, even though it may be that its normal life cycle has come to an end, it is still worthy of consideration as a symbolic communication.

If you look at it symbolically just as a matter of fact, then you are that much farther ahead in the pursuit of Self mastery.

The areas that most appliances are found in the house are the kitchen, laundry room and the bathroom, and they seem to develop the most problems in the least amount of time.

The kitchen represents sustenance. It can also represent family dining and those emotions; also friendly chats, social gathering. Depending upon what goes wrong in the kitchen it may deal in some degree with food preparation, which affects sustenance. If the refrigerator goes bad, there is a problem that, conceivably, what you have stored may deteriorate or rot. Now, take that thought and project into other aspects of what is going on in your life. It may symbolize that what you have confidence in, what think is going to sustain or support you, may be in danger of not being there for you.

Dishwasher malfunctions may indicate that there is a difficulty in cleansing something, dealing with material sustenance. Because if you ultimately cannot clean your dishes, then you have nothing to eat off of, which implies something else altogether; that which is providing you sustenance may be in question or danger.

Another item that malfunctions in the kitchen is the stove, the next major appliance, in which case you are talking about preparation. There may be something faulty in one's preparation with an upcoming project that could provide sustenance, provide the ability to bring nutrients into the system in a more assimilatable way. Sustenance has many ways of being provided.

The other thing that could go wrong in the kitchen is a lack of water. For those who live off of a well, that is easy to see. Lack of water could mean that there is a lack of life, a lack of material sustenance, the potential of something coming to an end, something being disrupted. There is something that is going to need additional effort or work to continue the flow. Do not forget that water is symbolic of your material life. This includes financial considerations.

One of the causes of a loss of water could be broken pipes; water cut off because of a lack of payment; it could also be that the well has run dry. In a situation like that, one has to question what it was that kept the well full, which could be the well of money, of peace, the well of comfort within the material, things of that nature.

Another area of the house that is affected by water flow is the bathroom. In this case, what you are looking at is a lack of cleansing in the material plane of obsolete thoughts and toxins. Again, from a different point of view, money and material sustenance provide the opportunity for cleansing.

Often, to go into a cleansing cycle of sorts means the willingness to give up certain things. The best way to give something up is from a position of strength, not that you are in dire need of it, but that you can give it up and do not need it for your daily sustenance and maintenance.

The term sustenance should not be confused with simple food consumption, because symbolically foods are thoughts; air, for instance, is necessary for sustenance, it is symbolic of spiritual thoughts. Water, which is also required for sustenance, is symbolic of the material plane.

In the bathroom a stopped up toilet would indicate an inability to cleanse. Stuff is backing up on you. The same thing could be said for a backed up septic tank. What is it that you cannot get free of? What is it that you are getting more and more immersed in that is of an unpleasant nature and you can not seem to flush away and get rid of?

Ark

It serves as a vessel that floats on the water and carries cargo. Depending upon the context in which it is seen or experienced, it could be a safe position from which to weather an emotional storm. If that storm is not understood it will manifest as an accident or physical symptom or condition.

In what way are you using an ark? Are you a passenger? What is the nature of the cargo? This, too, is a vehicle of expression.

Arms and Legs

The arms add additional strength and mobility to those things you handle, while the legs add strength and mobility to the support system, as well as to your ability to aspire. See also Right and Left for understandings as to what is going on.

Assets

In the physical/material realm they represent security. It is a false sense of security. The only true asset you have is your faith in yourself. This is built upon your experiences that have built courage and confidence within you, as well as the knowledge that you are never placed in a situation that you cannot master.

Astrology

Astrology is the study and ability to "read the stars." In truth, it is really the planets that are being looked at. Astrology knows where the planets are in relationship to each other. Stars are different. They can be a symbolic of different things.

There are always two ways to look at everything. One is the Universal Perspective. The other, and more important, is the PEA, the personal emotional association. Of course, the PEA is the most important perspective to attain and maintain. Universally, stars would be insights and inspiration, especially in doubt.

Think of night as a time of preparation. As you are sleeping, your mind is reexamining the stimuli you encountered during the day. The stimuli have triggered certain concepts, which, in turn, have started certain patterns of behavior in motion.

Stars do not light up the night sky. If you have ever been out in desert country or on the ocean far away from land and you looked up at the black expanse, it is just phenomenal. There are millions of stars. It is like saying there are a million insights and understandings within and without if you can just perceive them with clarity.

You never see a star clearly; it just cannot be done with the naked eye. Sometimes it is that way with an insight. When you are looking into your own doubt and uncertainty, you may get a glimmer, an outline, you may get a speck of truth, but to see the whole truth is going to take a much deeper focus. If you follow your insights and understandings, these little fragments of light, you will find your path, and that is what a ship's captain does when he uses the stars for guidance.

You are the captain of your ship trying to navigate through life, and that is what the sea is symbolic of, material reality, life. So, if you use the stars as guidance, then you are back to astrology; the cycles never end.

It may take a telescope to look outside of Self and, more importantly, it will take a microscope to look within.

B

Baby/Babies

Babies can represent many things, such as responsibilities; an immature form of expression; the result of creative expression. Are you a parent or a babysitter, a nurse or doctor taking care of babies?

It is essential to understand on a personal level what children mean to you.

Balls

These have different meanings depending upon the type of ball it is. Each would represent a different form of expression for you based on your involvement with the sport or event that the particular ball represents.

In addition to sports, balls can be used for bearings. They make things move easier, when greased even smoother and faster. What may be going on that needs greasing? What could bounce out of your hands? Think in all different ways when you seek to understand a symbol on emotional levels.

Banana peel

First and foremost is the fact that the peel is protective. That raises questions as to what or who you are trying to protect yourself from. If stepped upon, you could lose your balance and could cause yourself pain and discomfort. What is going on that could cause you to lose your balance?

Another interesting thing about a banana peel is that it gives you an external visualization of an internal process. The banana is turning to sugar inside the peel. You know the banana is going bad by looking at the outside. If a banana peel is brown, you are not going to eat it, or you will know what you are dealing with on the inside when you do peel it.

What is your mind trying to tell you? Do you need to peel something back in order to prevent it from going bad?

Bandana

See Headband.

Banner

Banners are used to make statements. What does the banner say? Where is it displayed? This, too, will give you some insight to what is going on.

Remember that nothing stands alone. You have to reconstruct the symbolic interpretations in order to get the most comprehensive picture.

Baseball Bat

This, too, is a form of expression. The fact that it is phallic in shape tells you that it refers to your expression of manhood. "Manhood" simply means that it is the way you personally express yourself, regardless of whether you are male or female. "Manhood" may imply both genders.

Are you sports-minded? Involved in baseball? What associations do you come up with when you think baseball bat? Is it a protective device? Do you use it to make a statement of who you are?

Basements

Sometimes there are basements in homes. These can be used for the same purpose as dens and family rooms. They can be paneled and made into a family room or TV room or an entertainment center.

The other side of that is that the basement could be a place of detainment, punishment, the mundane, or the washer/dryer. The basement could be an area of expression because it is where you have your workbench.

The basement also represents the subconscious, as does the bedroom. The basement, because it is below ground, is where the symbolism comes from.

Depending on what takes place here, it may also give one insight, certainly when interpreting a situation in life or a dream.

Bathroom

The bathroom, which can also sometimes be attached to the bedroom, is symbolic of cleansing. In reality that is exactly what you do in that room. You eliminate the wastes of your body as well as cleanse the exterior.

Each of those transactions within themselves has major symbolic significance. Obviously, cleansing the body speaks in terms of cleansing past man-made concepts from the Self. Washing the external is also removing toxins and creating a Self that is fresh and new, scraping off all the old, as well as those negative thoughts (bacteria), that dwell on the skin.

By reducing the numbers of potential invaders, you reduce the potentiality of being negatively affected through imposition and feelings of being overwhelmed. These are emotional feelings that manifest symbolically in different arenas within life. Fundamentally, they are emotional issues.

Bats

These creatures are nocturnal forms of thoughts. For their sustenance, they seek out insects, predominately mosquitoes, which are symbolic of petty annoyances. The fact that bats live in caves, symbolic of safe, deep, hidden or secluded dwelling places in the subconscious, tells you that there are thoughts that are always at work seeking to discover the annoyances that manifest in your periods of doubt.

Consider that evening time is a time of preparation for the morrow and, if you are not prepared with understanding the forces/energies that you will be facing and dealing with, you will respond to them from a position of doubt versus a position of strength. When that happens, it will be your patterns of behavior that will be responding in an automatic fashion.

Bats, from an alternate point of view, are a collective society. They band together for security. You never see a bat alone. When they take off, they do so in a group. In spite of their blindness, they have developed other senses to help them feed and nourish themselves and grow. The fact that they eat insects demonstrates that if we were to incorporate bat-thinking into our reality, we could say that the bats are here to teach us that even though we may be blind to the petty annoyances because of our emotions; if we were to listen intently we might hear them. We might hear the little jabs, the little cuts, the little innuendoes, the little suggestions, all those things that we do not see. The façade looks wonderful, "Oh honey, I love you. Everything is great! Geez, what kind of lousy haircut is that?" You have to learn to be able to hear; to have eyes that see and ears that hear[15]. Bats are here to teach us that, through learning to hear and keeping your thoughts collected, you can sustain yourself in the darkest of all situations.

Beard

Here you have two very different interpretations from the Universal perspective. A beard could be a way of hiding or altering your image. Another is the image of wisdom, sage, authority or mature expression.

Bed

Beds can present many different symbolic definitions. One is escape because you can crawl into bed and shut out the world. Inactivity is also associated with the bed from that perspective.

Two, it is a place of preparation because when you sleep you prepare for tomorrow's journey through physical rejuvenation and emotionally through the interpretation and understanding of your dreams.

Third, it could be an area of expression. Some people earn a living in bed. Another aspect is the role that it plays in creating children.

Children are generally conceived in bed, so it is creative from that aspect and also a form of expression.

Bedroom

The bedroom is symbolic of the subconscious mind because this is where you prepare for the next day. This is where you sleep and dream, even when you do not remember doing so. This is the pause in a cycle. Every cycle is defined as an action and a pause. The bedroom is where preparation takes place for the activities of tomorrow.

Dreams tell you the patterns of behavior at work so that you can have a handle on them. When you interpret your dreams in the morning, you know where you are in the cycle of a pattern of behavior. It will also show you how to handle the particular cycle and pattern,

Through dream interpretations you can go into the world from a position of strength and deal with the energies of life confronting you, knowing to some degree what some of the possibilities and the probabilities are based on where you are in the flow on the pattern of behavior. Now you have the opportunity to create new potentialities, thus you end up elevating yourself by being in control over your patterns.

Symbols also help the individual to see the root causes, the concepts behind the patterns. When you look long enough and hard enough you will come to an understanding. This is another beauty of symbols in dreams because it is a constant form of communication to help you in your questioning process.

The bedroom can represent other things too It could be a place of punishment or discomfort. If somebody has sexual issues and they are forced to perform, then the bedroom may represent imposition, punishment, confinement, and imprisonment.

On the other side of the coin, it could be creativity. Again, one must always go back to the PEA in order to understand what it means to the Self.

Bee sting

If you are allergic to bees, a sting could be fatal. For those folks, a bee may represent threats or death.

Fundamentally, bees are known for working and living in social consciousness, a collective consciousness, a welfare-of-the-whole as opposed to the "what about me" approach to life. Each class of bee has a particular function.

Because the bee makes honey, when they appear in your dreams it could indicate that there is something in a current transaction that you are involved in, something small that has the potential of turning out sweet, something that may or may not have been an irritant.

They could represent an opportunity if approached from a collective, social, organized fashion. Bees could also represent aggression because of their stinging capabilities. They could represent an irritant, a threat, or an attack.

Do not forget that if you have been stung by a bee, or this occurs in your dream, there will be discomfort. So, there could be an uncomfortable situation, and although small, it could become major.

Bells

Joyful noises, communications; bells provide a sound. It could be joyful to the ear, or distressing. Bells are also used for alarms, either for awakening or for reminding. They could also be for identifying location, like a cow's bell, so you know where something is.

Bells may be a way of drawing your attention to something so you have an opportunity to maximize the potential of it or to minimize the potential, depending on whether it is going to be beneficial or harmful.

Between

Sometimes in dreams you may find yourself between this and that, which may stop your forward motion. Feeling caught or stuck between two things would be an indication of feeling trapped, stymied, or stifled.

When I think of stymied, I think more along an intellectual line, and stifled more along a physical line. Between could also indicate the need for a decision to be made.

Birds

Birds are symbolic of spiritual thoughts because they dwell in the sky, the home of God. Air and sky are both symbolic of the Spiritual plane of consciousness. Birds are symbolic of thoughts that are spiritual in nature with aspirations; your spiritual thoughts.

Each type of bird will offer a different symbolic meaning based on many factors such as species, color, size, habitat, and the nature of the bird itself.

Is bird watching a hobby or profession? Other thoughts need to be considered.

Your faith in yourself will produce a large branch that becomes shelter for the birds of heaven. Your thoughts could be sheltered in your Self faith because you know you have a working faith; you know, "I can do this, I am mastery in action".

Black

This color usually indicates doubt at work. An example of this is found in the expression, "black mood." When a person is in this frame of mind it is because they are uncomfortable or uncertain about where they are in a given situation. It can also represent a time of preparation, such as night when dreaming can help you prepare for the upcoming day.

It is also symbolic of a lack of or very negative emotions, a "black heart." It is also the absence of Light.

Black & Blue

These two colors manifesting at the same time in the same area indicate soreness, a hurt, and could be the result of conflict. Where they manifest in the body will tell you where it is that you hurt when you understand the symbology of the part of the body that you damaged.

By whom or what and in what way do you feel "beat up?"

Bladder

The bladder is nothing more than a holding sac, a temporary storage container. It is designed to retain the liquid wastes that the kidneys filter out of the bloodstream. Upon command, the bladder will empty.

The bladder is a storage area for emotional wastes, also symbolic of control and maturity. When you learned how to control your bladder you stepped into a new realm of growth and maturity. It is interesting that as you continue on this path of maturity the muscles that control the ability to eliminate seem to break down and there is leakage. The reason that this usually happens is because of poor mineralization of the entire body. This affects the ability of the muscles that control that process to function. Any problem here would indicate that something is amiss in the cleansing systems.

Blonde

This color, like all colors, implies a particular level of thought. In today's society, one of the connotations of being blonde is lacking intelligence. It is also representative of, "Look at me" for those who want to be seen as, "Blondes have more fun." That, itself, raises questions as to the person's definition of fun.

The true interpretation will again depend upon your personal association with who, as a blonde, was influential in your life, in either a positive or negative way.

Blood

Blood is symbolic of the spiritual life that exists within. Almost all living things have that commonality; a liquid that flows through the system carrying nutrients and building material, as well as carrying away the waste and debris. That is why the Bible tells us, in Deuteronomy[16], to remove the blood before eating any animal.

Blue

This color is symbolic of Spirit or heaven. The sky is blue and is where God is perceived to dwell. On an emotional level, this will indicate sadness, a feeling of being down.

Blues is also a style of music. How does that relate to your dream or vision?

Books

These provide information, knowledge, pleasure, and escape. They can also represent expression, especially if you are a poet or writer.

Bottle

Bottles are containers and, depending upon the type of bottle (soda, milk, juice, etc.) will determine what aspect of your life it is relevant to.

You have different associations with the contents of each of those bottles, as well as the fact that you may have an association with bottles altogether. The type of bottle will influence the Universal interpretation while the PEA will provide greater insight for interpretation. Examples might be: milk, which would be indicative of seeking mother's approval; alcohol indicates a desire to party, be social or to escape.

You could work in a glass factory, which would indicate that the bottles are tied into your expression. The point is that the bottle, which fundamentally can act as a container, brings up the question: What are you containing? What do you want to contain? What do you want to put a lid on and in what arena of your life?

Another aspect of the interpretation would be based on whether or not the bottle contained any liquid or other substance and how full or empty it is in your dream.

Boulders

See Rocks and Stones.

Bra

A supportive device related to expression. The breasts represent the expression of manhood for women. Size infers the level of depth of the concepts related to nurturing, as well as sexual expression. They can also represent the degree of self-acceptance, as well as the desire to be seen and noticed.

Difficulties here represent conflict within between how you think you should be as a women and how you actually are and expected to be, based on external demands. This is especially true in relationships.

Brain

The brain represents the spiritual domain because it is within the brain that the mind dwells. Depending upon how this appears in a dream, it may give you an indication that more faith is required or more understanding is essential in whatever the matter is that you are confronting.

Branch

Generally, a branch is a limb from a tree. On one level you would benefit from looking at what is going on in your material life, your means of sustenance. What is happening in your ability to support yourself?

The reason you are taking that approach is because a tree is symbolic of the material plane. It takes from the ground and through the process of photosynthesis it releases oxygen back into the air.

The question comes up: Where am I, "out on a limb?"

Break-in

Breaking in denotes loss because the end result is that you will be deprived of something. If you are experiencing a break-in, you have to question where the break-in is occurring. Is it your home, car, place of business?

Each one of these arenas has a different symbology, although car and business relate together in the sense that both are vehicles of expression. The home is a base of security.

The question arises: In what way is your expression under attack? In what ways are you vulnerable to attack? Why would you bring an attack on? Remember that you are constantly co-creating your reality, so no matter what happens – good, bad, indifferent, ugly – you are partially the cause because you are asking for it and receiving it. Question what is going on and why that would be a part of your experience.

Breasts

The size of breasts is an indication of how a woman thinks about herself. It reflects concepts as to the role as a woman. They are also indicative of ideas surrounding motherhood. See also Bra.

Bricks/Stones

Bricks, stones and rocks are all one in the same. They can represent aggression or defenses. You could use them to attack another, and another could use them to defend him/herself either by throwing them at you or erecting a barrier with them, as in a wall.

Because stones are defenses, they can be removed through understanding of the concepts that support them so you do not feel the need to defend that arena of yourself because you understand who you are in that regard.

Sometimes, if the stones, rocks or bricks have a particular color or hue to them, you may want to look up the symbology of the colors. If they are bright red, you know there is anger or energy afoot. If they are yellow, proceed with caution. If they are orange, seek to understand.

Look at all aspects of a symbol in order to get the depth of everything it could possibly communicate to you.

Bright colors

Flashy, social butterfly; when you have an individual that shows up in your dreams or visions in bright colors, you know that this is a person that is saying, "Look at me. Do you see me?"

On one level, bright colors indicate a flag of sorts, such as feelings of inadequacy, in that the bright colors are used to overcompensate.

They can also represent good feelings, joy, happiness and pleasure.

Bronchial Tubes

When the bronchial tubes are congested or inflamed it represents conflict within. Whenever you are dealing with bronchial issues, especially bronchitis, the immediate thought that should be considered and examined is Self-doubt. The lungs are symbolic of spirit because they bring in oxygen (spirit), which is where spirit dwells.

Any issues with the lungs, bronchial tubes or nasal passages relate to doubt in Self and the inability to draw on your internal working faith, your faith in your Self.

Look around and see what is going on. What situations, conditions or events are causing you to have doubt in your Self that would choke you up and make you congested? What is making you feel overwhelmed?

Brown

Earth; grounded; rooted; sustenance; soil for vegetables; mundane. See Colors.

Buffeted

If you are buffeted by the wind, it is slight impedance, a little bit of resistance. Where are you headed that there could be some resistance to whatever it is you need to do?

Or, you could have been Jimmy Buffeted, in which case you have been made mellow. Or you could have been Warren Buffeted, in which case you have been made rich. Enjoy them all.

Bullets

Bullets, like other symbolic physical manifestations of manhood; i.e., arrows and spears, represent two things almost immediately. One is aggression, which could lead to threats and eventual annihilation. The other is defense. A third interpretation could be sustenance.

If someone knows that you have a loaded gun, they may not come after you. It is like the nuclear arms theory. If each country has them, and they know we have them, they will not attack us and we will not attack them because we know they have them.

Bullets fall into the same realm as arrows and spears; however, all of them could also be for sustenance because you can use them to hunt. If you are a hunter, they have a different meaning to you entirely. This is something where you would have to try to understand if there is a personal emotional association with bullets.

For example: you found your father's bullets and he smacked you because you were messing around with the bullets and he knows that is dangerous. You do not know that; you are too young to know, but he got angry. Therefore, the bullets could represent anger or aggression.

Bulls

Bulls represent power, authority, and aggression. They may also represent sustenance from the point of view that you raise cattle and they are essential to grow the herd.

Bullies

We all know bullies. They are the people who are always attacking someone smaller, younger or less powerful than they are. When bullies do that, they are really coming from a place of fear and doubt and the only way they can make themselves feel better is by attacking others.

When these energies show up in your dreams, visions or in life, the question that needs to be asked is: Why are you drawing this energy to you? Why are you drawing an aggressive personality or aggressive energy toward you? This could also be energy of authority and maybe you feel that you are being bullied.

Bus

As a passenger, you are at the mercy and skill of the driver. You are subject to the concepts of whoever is in the driver's seat. Buses, cars, trains and planes all take you from place to place. The goings and comings could be tied into expression on a personal level; work, pleasure or escape. See also Vehicles of Expression.

Business Endeavor

To have this type of scenario appear in a dream could indicate the ability or need to understand the energies at work and guide them to some degree. Depending upon your role within that environment, it will give you some insight as to aspects of your expression.

Whatever your function is in an office, warehouse or retail environment, it is part of your sustenance. You could say that it symbolically represents material sustenance in the material plane, as well as its personal aspects of expression for you.

In seeking to understand why you would be in a business situation not part of your norm is to understand the nature of that business and the relationship it has to your sustenance.

Butterfly

Metamorphosis; being totally helpless and then being able to fly free; totally grounded; going within to become new entity; things of beauty.

Buttocks

These represent sitting, inactivity. It can also mean resting or discomfort (as in a pain in the butt). Who or what is a pain in the butt? What is the best way to deal with it?

Are you resting on your laurels? Do you need to get off your buttocks and be about whatever your calling is, whatever it is you are here to do, which is first and foremost to understand your Self then develop your gifts and give back to humanity?

This area of the body should also be considered symbolically from the attraction/sexual perspective.

C

Calcium

Calcium represents strength, you need it to build bone and teeth and it is involved with multiple biochemical transactions such as the contractions of your muscles.

For greater insight on all of the minerals, as well as health, diseases and conditions, read the "Health and Disease Symbology Handbook."

Called

Called is a word implying a spiritual/religious endeavor; "It is my calling. It is what I am here to do. I have been called to duty to do this." If this is something you are experiencing, the questions are: What is it? Where is the call coming from? What is the intent of the call? How do you feel about it? Is it in harmony with you, and which you is it in harmony with – your ego you or your true Self you, which you may not yet fully know and understand?

Camel

The camel is considered the "ship of the desert." It can traverse dunes of the sand sea easier than any other creature on the planet.

On some levels, camels represent the ability to traverse that which is difficult to pass over or travel through. It also represents the ability to move forward without the need for sustenance, which is not completely accurate. However, it is based on the symbology that once a camel's thirst is quenched, it can go for days without requiring water. This is an element of endurance and acclamation to one's environment.

Water is symbolic of material life. On some levels you could say sustenance. In a dream or experience, it says that on some levels you have within you the ability to do this upcoming project/event. You just have to take on the attitude of a camel. You do not require much external sustenance or support. You have the power and strength within you and, as difficult as the terrain may be for others in terms of footing, you can do this.

In order to ensure success in that, you have to look at the other symbols in the dream and tie it all together.

Car

The car is symbolic of expression. You use your expression as a vehicle to take you from place to place. That is what a car does. The car is a personal form of expression. Symbolically you need to examine the type of car. Is it a coupe, convertible, SUV, a minivan or a truck? Next examine the color of the vehicle and incorporate its symbology to achieve a greater understanding of the energies at work.

Is the vehicle color red? This can represent an active and passionate person; blue a spiritual person; green healing, calming, soothing; brown earthy; black doubt, gray also doubt; white can be doubt but also faith. Again, you must go back to personal emotional associations because the PEA is always the most important, which cannot be emphasized enough.

As a passenger, you are at the mercy of the driver. You are subject to the concepts of whoever is in the driver's seat.

In examining your own vehicle it will give you some insight as to aspects of your personality and responsibility levels as well as your desire level, which may or may not be present. See also Vehicles of Expression.

Car: Parked

If your car is parked in a dream, in a vision, then your expression, your mode of expression, your feelings of being able to express yourself are also parked, inactive, or inoperable. They are waiting for you to put in the key, the insight, the understanding to turn on, to allow the juice to flow, give it life, give it spark, get the engine cranked, take it out of park and put it in gear.

Carriage

There are many types of carriages that come to mind, the first being the traditional horse and buggy style carriage. You can take a carriage ride around Central Park in New York, ride around the French Quarter in New Orleans or a ride around historic Philadelphia. The question becomes when was the last time you took such a ride and where was it and what transpired?

You may drive a carriage and, therefore, sustenance is involved. You may care for the horses or equipment. In what way do you relate to a carriage of that style or type?

The baby carriage: are you pushing it or are you being pushed in it? The carriage of this type would indicate an immature expression. If you are doing the pushing then it could represent responsibility. See also Vehicles of Expression.

Cat

Cats give the appearance of being independent when, in truth, they are co-dependent on the person that feeds them. Although cats do appear not to need you or want your attention, they show a different side when they do want something from you. Who is it that seems to be independent of you yet requires and seeks your help in matters?

Are you an independent person or is there a tendency to be co-dependent? What other symbols are in the dream and, when you reconstruct it from the symbolic perspective, what is the cat saying to you? How does the presence of the cat influence your interpretation?

They are not necessarily friendly. They also give off an air of indifference.

The breed of cat would also be symbolic.

Cattle

Cattle represent sustenance, convenience, and responsibility. It is convenience in the sense that their meat provides sustenance, however their hide is used for the manufacturing of shoes, clothing and other forms of accessories.

Cattle can also be a material expression in the sense that you may earn your living that is in some way connected to cattle. That may also imply a personal emotional association that should be examined.

Caves

Caves represent withdrawal, very much like basements. They are the subconscious. In this case it is not so much delving into the subconscious to explore the basement, but more hiding in a cave, like a bear hibernating in the winter.

You could do cave diving and exploring as part of your expression or a hobby and something you enjoy doing. You may also have had an experience in a cave, whether good, bad or indifferent, which is the emotional association to draw upon.

Symbolic of safe, deep, hidden or secluded dwelling places in the subconscious.

Chairs

Chairs represent multiple things and here is a situation where you must revert back to your personal emotional association in order to get the best definition of what being in a chair might mean to you in a dream sequence.

For instance chairs can represent sustenance, sitting at the kitchen table, a dining room table. It could represent relaxation, sitting in a lean-back chair, a recliner, any of those types of chairs where you can elevate your feet and just relax.

It could be a desk chair, which would indicate expression, what you sit on to do your creative work. It could be an imposition; it is where you had to sit when you were made to do your homework. It could be punishment, where you were made to sit during time-out.

A chair can also represent affection. It is where your mother or grandmother held you. There are multiple definitions for a chair, but you must seek out your personal emotional association with it.

Children

Children can represent different things. They can represent immature expression and other aspects of Self, especially in dreams. The aspect of immaturity is that of a chronological nature. The other is of an emotional nature.

What I mean by chronological is social adaptability. This is where the social Self comes into play. Do not forget that you are instructed to become as children in order to enter into Heaven[17], indicating defenselessness.

The questions that arise are: In what ways are you not a child? In what ways do you relate to the children you have? When are you a child? When is that triggered? When is that a symbol of a pattern-influenced thinking?

Children's Rooms

Rooms have many different symbolic interpretations based on the particular function that the room serves. A child's room could mean an immature sense of being. It can also be a form of security or it may even represent confinement.

You need to ask how this may apply to your life and place in the dream. Look at what is currently going on in your life and see how this might apply. These rooms can also indicate an immature aspect of self; an immature perception and immature feelings. All of these would be in regard to whatever is going on in your life at the moment.

Chin

The chin represents an aspect of image. There are many sayings related to the chin. Here are a few of those expressions: "Chin up," "Take it on the chin," "Leads with his chin;" all of those relate to presenting a particular image to the world with a particular attitude.

There are two questions that arise. What were you thinking about? What were you headed toward? What were you coming from? You were obviously walking in a particular direction with a particular thought in your mind, or going from one experience to another experience.

Christ –Self

Jesus is symbolic of what all of mankind is capable of attaining in the way of consciousness and expression of the God Force that dwells within. Jesus is symbolic of one reaching Divine Love, total Self-acceptance; this is expressed as achieving God-head; Nirvana. This is when one becomes in tune with the Creative Continuum called God and is able to manifest the spiritual gifts that dwell within.

These spiritual gifts are attributes to help facilitate man's journey through the material plane so that your soul can be freed from this energy web called the material plane and move on to a greater level of understanding that would bring you closer in harmony with God.

Chorus

Think of harmony and balance because choruses are generally one of two things: the vocal or the physical, such as dancing. In both instances, the entire performance is balanced for the musical piece at hand, as well as harmonized through the physical movements and synchronicity of the voices.

If you find yourself in a chorus, this would bring to mind seeking balance and harmony. Did you participate in a chorus? Was it ever a part of your life? It could be taking you back to a particular cycle or a particular desire. How does that relate to what you are going through now?

In addition to balance and harmony, it also relates to relationships. The commonality there is that they all want to be part of a chorus. What are the things you want to be a part of or that would be in your soul/spirit's growth interest to harmonize with?

It could be telling you that you are going into a cycle of seeking and to be open and aware. Dreams are both retro-cognitive and pre-cognitive. They will draw on past experiences using that language of experience that you have made emotional associations with and will project them into the future. In that way you can see what upcoming energy lies ahead of you. By being forewarned you can be forearmed, and you can make the necessary changes to avoid whatever it is the pre-cognitive symbol told you, which will retro-cognitively reflect a particular pattern of behavior.

Church

It is a house of worship. The questions that arise when this is in your dreams or visions are: What is your association with the church? Does it represent authority? Is it comfort? Was it imposition? Was it fear? Was it obligation? Was it social? Was it learning? Was it satisfying? What does the church represent to you?

When you find yourself in that environment, depending upon the other events involved, it is worthy of questioning. There is always the possibility that a church was not your place of worship. Even with that in mind seek to understand your thoughts and feelings about churches.

Circular Saw

A circular saw in dreams or visions can represent a vehicle of expression. It could also be part of a hobby, but would still be an aspect of the expression. It could represent a thing of danger; it may have hurt someone in the past.

It could also be an aid or an ally because it can help you get things done, depending on what your profession is.

Saws are used in everything from butchering animals to cutting stones for housing. Basically, it is a tool of expression and you have to consider how it applies to you on a personal basis.

Circulatory System

The circulatory system is present throughout the body, with blood that flows through it carrying nourishment to every cell. The blood also removes waste material generated by the cells, keeping them in a clean environment. This cleansing process, along with the immune system, prevents bacteria from gaining a foothold in the body, which in turn prevents diseases.

Blood is symbolic of the spiritual life that exists within all living things. That is why the Bible tells us, in Deuteronomy[18], to remove the blood before eating any animal.

The blood carries nutrients, which are symbolic of thought energies, from your lungs and intestines, carrying them throughout the body. Your food (thoughts in the form of vegetables, fruit, fowl, meat, or junk food) can nourish, cleanse and heal, or they can clog and destroy you. What is your diet like? What thoughts or external belief system are you tied into? Does it feed you? Does it answer your questions?

Closets

Closets are a place to put things out of view, to hang clothes and to hide things. It could also be a place of containment, a utility place, a place of terror, or an are of punishment.

Clothing

Clothes represent personal image and status. They can also represent defenses. It depends on your association with the type of clothes being seen or experienced in your dreams, visions and daily life.

If you are a clothes horse and you always need to buy clothes to be this particular persona, then the question comes up, "Can you let go of clothes easily?" Can you give up a particular vision of yourself?

Cleaning

In your dream, if you find yourself cleaning floors, which are symbolic of foundation, questions have to be asked as to why you think it is not clean. Do you think it could ever be clean enough? In what area is it? Which room do you find yourself cleaning? What is going on that is making you think that the room or floors are dirty?

The other part of cleansing is the internal cleansing and eliminating toxins and waste from the body.

Coat

Coats represent protection from the elements. They could also represent image. The coat you choose to wear represents what you choose to say to the world. There are certain looks that are totally functional, but there are other looks that make statements. Look at your coats. What do they say about you?

In what way do you need protection and what are the elements you wish to be protected from? What is an element? Some people will immediately think of wind, rain, sleet, hail, sun, earth or water. But attitudes are also elements. Energies are elements.

In addition to providing protection, coats provide warmth. If you find yourself in a dream where it is mid-summer and you are requiring coats for protection and warmth, then what is going on around you and in what way do you feel left out in the cold? In what way have you been chilled, and by whom?

Cockroaches

Cockroaches are generally associated with filth and debris. Cockroaches could also be a symbol of feeling that one is in a cycle of poverty. You could be cockroach free and all of a sudden you wake up and you have three of them, what is going on?

Cockroaches have survived many different environments over the centuries. This leads to another symbolic interpretation: endurance, adaptability and surviving the elements. You could examine the word element, because what are the elements that are involved in your life?

You may think fire, wind, hail, storm, but elements could also be emotional states that you could be going through, so there is another avenue of thought to pursue.

Cockroaches are symbols of unkemptness, not necessarily sloppy or lazy, but not necessarily adamant either about keeping a clean house, so it draws cockroaches. They are annoyances and they are dirty and leave a dirty trail behind, which can contaminate food.

When cockroaches show up, you have to ask: What is your relationship to cockroaches? What memories does it stir or arouse? What are the associations? What and who are the cockroaches in your life now that are leaving little messes behind that could be contaminating and polluting your life, your journey?

Colors

Colors add dimension to every symbol. By applying the symbolic interpretation of a color will provide a deeper more comprehensive understanding of the symbol being examined.

Red signifies danger, anger and passion. That is why the hearts are always red. Stop signs and warning signs are also red.

Now, I am giving you the universal perspective and not the personal emotional association because you may have a different association with the color red. You could have had a red blanket as a child and that was your security.

Green is healing, calming, soothing and nurturing. The nurturing aspect derives from vegetables because they are predominately green. There is an expression in the health food industry: fruits cleanse, vegetables heal. Money is also green.

Purple is considered to be symbolic of royalty because most of the kings and queens were clothed in purple.

Yellow is caution before proceeding; it implies learning all that you can about the situation you are involved with, the energies at hand. Buddhist monks wear yellow-orange robes; that goes along the lines of seeking.

Blue is spiritual and it also represents material life because of its association with the color of water, which is symbolic of the material plane.

Blue is also very cool to the touch. All colors actually have a vibration and feel that you could train your mind to sense through your fingertips. You can learn to become relaxed enough do a meditation and run your fingers over colors and in time you will be able to discern what color you are feeling at the time.

Brown always makes me think of being grounded. It is the color of the earth. It is also the color of other things that are not nearly as pleasant.

It depends on the other aspects of the dream and what is going on in order to gain greater clarity as to what brown can represent.

Also, it could represent something barren, dead, in the sense that brown dirt is not always able to produce life. Again, you have to go back and find what the circumstances are in the environment as seen or experienced.

Black would be doubt and fear and it could also be preparation. Black signifies doubt because it is difficult to see in it.

When it comes to looking into doubt, you need to look into the doubt within your Self. What are you doubtful about? What are the concepts in your subconscious mind that tell you that you cannot do this or that or you do not have the ability, authority, right, know-how, knack, intelligence, looks, etc.?

Gray also represents doubt, but not nearly as solidly as black, because doubt can lead to fear. Uncertainty, which gray also represents, is a little bit of doubt with a little bit of working faith mixed together. So, there is an uncertainty as to whether or not whatever is at hand can be done.

Communication

Communication is mutually seeking an insight and understanding that will lead to harmony, and I think in politics and law the goal is to win the argument, vanquish the opponent, gain the upper hand and gain power. And that is really not what communication is about.

Computer

Computers can represent different things; fundamentally it is a matter of outreach or expression and they can be used for communicating on multiple levels. It could be a tool for learning.

The application of the computer will influence the symbology. If you use it for writing, homework and communicating with others and it malfunctions, it could be an indication that something is brewing that is going to hamper your ability to communicate or the ability to express, the ability to gain knowledge, and the ability to do your job.

Obviously, there is something going on from that perspective. It could also be used for business, in which case if you cannot control your inventory to invoices, etc., then it may affect your sustenance, as well as your expression. See also Vehicles of Expression.

Couch

A couch could be for relaxation, and relaxation could also indicate withdrawal or avoidance. The couch could be your favorite place to nap and rejuvenate your energy levels. It could be where you and your significant other cuddle so it could be expression, romance and it could also represent security. Again, there are multiple definitions.

Crab

Like most crustaceans, crabs are bottom-feeders. In that regard, they help to keep the ocean clean, which is one of the reasons why, from biblical dietary law, man is not supposed to eat them[19].

If a crab ever bit you, they could represent aggression on a personal level. If you like to eat them, they could represent a good time, an emotional connection, a fond memory or a horrible memory. It depends on what your association is with them. Once again, you are back to the personal emotional association.

Cream

Sustenance; cream of the crop; the very best; rich. Those are the immediate thoughts that come to mind. Here, again, one needs to look at this from a personal emotional perspective and understand your symbolic association.

What does cream represent to you? If you are born on a farm, it is one thing. If you do a lot of baking, it is another thing. If this appears in a dream or a vision, or if you keep seeing it repeatedly in ads, it is your mind's way of saying, "What does cream represent to you?" Was it a treat like bananas and cream or cream pies? What is the association for you?

Crib

A crib represents different things. For a child it has one interpretation and for an adult it has another. Fundamentally, the crib is a bed and, as such, it represents recuperation and sexual expression.

If you dream of being in a crib you could be feeling immature, inadequate, feel that you are being treated like a baby, confined or imprisoned. It could also be precognitive of having a child soon. That would bring up the question of expression because children are forms of expression of the adult, which would bring to mind the kind of child you may be inclined to raise.

The more you know your Self, the greater the guide you can be to the soul that is entering into that body.

Crickets

Crickets are insects that are active in the evening with their noise indicating their presence. They can stimulate fear in those who are afraid of insects. You have to understand your feelings about insects, and then narrow it down to crickets.

If you have lived in the city for your entire life, up to this moment, you may not have come in contact with one. If you live in the country, you may never have been able to get away from them or their noise. It is the noise that also may have some symbolic significance for you.

Crickets could also be food for pets. Again, you have to examine your relationship to these creatures and discover what they mean to you. Does it tell you that you need to be active at night? Are you utilizing your time effectively?

Crippled/Affliction

Symbols are symbols. That is why, when you look at the person who has a crippled leg, crippled arm, or the child that is born deformed, it is appropriate to say, "Wow, you really chose an interesting thing to learn this life cycle."

When this type of symbol appears in a dream, you have to look at what part of the body is affected, as well as which side. See body part symbolism and right and left side definitions for greater clarity. For a more detailed understanding, read the "Health and Disease Symbology Handbook," available at www. innerhealthbooks.com.

No matter what befalls anyone, you know that they have chosen it, they have created it through karma and patterns, and it is exactly what they need to understand and master in this life cycle. Whether or not they ever come to grips with their particular issue, they had their opportunity for mastery. They may not have seized it, but they had the opportunity.

Critters

Every single critter teaches us something if we understand how it lives, how it functions, how it hunts, the purpose it serves and how it is organized. Everything that is in the material plane is here for our illumination. Everything is here to help us master life. Every animal we dream about will teach us something if we examine how it lives and functions.

Crutches/Canes

Crutches and canes are aids for standing erect and personal mobility. Obviously, there is damage to one or both legs and possibly the hips, too. Maybe the person in the dream, you or someone else, is an amputee.

Crutches become an artificial means of support. They are not easy to navigate with, not easy to maintain balance with, and are very uncomfortable. Canes represent a softer application since they are used more for walking than support.

The question when either of these is present in a dream is: In what way are you being artificially supported? Why do you feel the need for that type of support?

If your right leg is broken, then there is an upcoming situation in which you lack faith in your Self as being able to deal with the situation effectively from a position of strength. If it is your left leg that is damaged, then there is something coming up, or you are currently dealing with, material sustenance.

If you have lost both legs, it indicates concepts that one is not strong enough to stand on one's own and, therefore, one becomes co-dependent.

Crystal

Crystals represent clarity. They also represent communication. This aspect goes back to the days of crystal radios.

They represent clarity because you can see through a crystal, as in crystal glassware. A crystal prism, when light passes through it, creates a rainbow effect. It can distort perception, also.

Crystals are also used by healers to convey healing power. They may have some metaphysical association for the individual who is experiencing crystals in dreams or visions. What do crystals represent for you? Are they part of your expression?

Cup

Cups are fundamentally a container, usually for drinking. What you are partaking of is something you need to be mindful of as well. Partaking could run the gamut of a material source of sustenance because from a cup you can drink water, soda, milk, smoothies, etc. Or it can be a form of transporting a small amount of something from one place to another? What is it that you feel needs to be transported?

From another perspective, what is it you would like to have more of? What do you want another cup of? What is it that a cup will suffice for or that you want to end up with?

Cushion

When you think of cushions, comfort immediately comes to mind. They can also be a source of protection if you find yourself surrounded by them. They can also be symbolic of being over-pressured or suppressed. As a child, someone could have put a bunch of pillows or cushions on someone and sat on them. Today, to that person cushions represent suppression, confinement and possibly imposition.

Cushions may also be symbolic of looking for a soft way out, a soft landing. Be aware that you may need to cushion a fall. There may be something brewing and you need to scan the horizon to see what energies are at work. When is it that you seek a soft, comfortable position, conceivably, an inactive position?

D

Dagger

The dagger, like all phallic symbols represent the expression of manhood. This statement also includes women as this is based on the Bible teaching: God created male and female[20].

If this symbol is prominent in your dream this leads you to question: How you are expressing yourself, what kind of attitude are you demonstrating in your daily life? Is someone else's expression of manhood an issue? First and foremost, always relate everything back to yourself.

Darkness

Symbolic of the unknown, darkness may represent the pause of a cycle. This is based on the fact that night precedes day[21]. At night every person dreams for the purpose of being prepared to deal with the forces of the upcoming day. Dreams are a time for preparation.

More often than not, darkness indicates an inability to see and understand the forces at work. It also denotes degrees of uncertainty, which is usually triggered by doubt and fear as well as depending upon how one feels about the dark.

Were you punished by being placed in a dark closet or room? Were you ever attacked in the dark? What experiences have you had that would create an emotional issue with being in the dark? How do they relate to the now?

Day

Day is symbolic of a cycle, as well as light and clarity. What is interesting is that if you go back to the bible, it always starts with evening and then daylight. Evening represents preparation. Day represents action. Evening can also represent doubt if you are not prepared.

A day cycle is a matter of a pause and an action. This is also stated in the Gospel According to Thomas[22].

Every action cycle is preceded by a pause, which gives you the opportunity to prepare for it so that you can go into it from a position of strength.

Deadbolt

A deadbolt is a particular style of lock. It is one that provides an extra sense of security. Once you deadbolt the door, you feel that you are in a more secure environment. It acts as a device to protect you from outside forces.

Depending upon which side of the deadbolt you are on, if it is keeping you out, then look about and see what or who is deterring your ability to enter into something or someone, or it could that you are being blocked from moving forward.

Examine the symbol from either of those perspectives to understand what you are trying to keep out or protect yourself from.

What are you trying to get into that seems to be locked down tight from your entering within? Could it be a particular person?

Detached

This is more of an emotional feeling than a physical detachment. However, if you have lost a limb the feelings and interpretations will be different. Detachment can be feeling out of sync with everything that is going on. There are other distractions that come along that can stimulate greater feelings of being detached.

This feeling can also represent "not belonging."

Dove

Doves are traditionally the symbol of peace. From a universal perspective they are symbolic of your lofty spiritual thoughts and ideals.

This following interpretation is from a study group I conducted. A dead dove was seen in front of a student's garage. Like all symbols it indicates an aspect of guidance on the energies that are active in her life at the moment.

In these types of situations you look at both the universal and the emotional personal relationship to the dove and the location.

The symbology of the garage can take on many different interpretations. For instance your garage is where you park your vehicle. And your vehicle is symbolic of your personal expression. If your car is in the garage then that is another aspect of the symbology that will lead to greater understanding.

Dead and death have their own interpretations. There are two ways to look at death. You can take the fearless approach through understanding and say, "Oh, death is just a doorway from this dimension to the next." That is all well and true. The other way is to think that death is the end. This could lead to feelings of fear because of the uncertainty or doubt.

When you look at death from the symbolic perspective you see it as the end of a cycle, which could be a life cycle; a transition; an event. It could also indicate rejection. For some death is an avenue of escape.

Once you are dead you are done. "I reject this whole thing, I am not going to deal with it any more, and I am out of here." It is worthwhile to mention that very few people die from old age. People die from failure of some part of one of the many systems, glands or organs that maintain the body.

Until you can come to the point where you are in such total control that you can lay the body down and say, "I am done with it, I do not need it anymore," there is the possibility that fear of the unknown can influence your thinking.

This dead dove symbol is symbolic that there is some particular thought that is being rejected or it is not coming to fruition. It does not have the wings or life to fly. There may be a lack of activity in some area.

If it is in, or in front of the garage, maybe you are seeking some kind of peaceful solution to a situation. Or, maybe you were seeking some kind of a peaceful idea or some kind of a harmonious solution to a situation that is involved with your expression on some lofty level.

Dead and Death

Both represent the same thing. They are the ending of a cycle. That interpretation can be applied to so many different things that you have to question what it is that could be coming to an end. What are you involved in? Was whatever you saw that was dead or dying on the right or the left side of where you were standing?

If it was the right side, know that there is an ending of a cycle that deals with personal power and faith in Self or an emotional cycle of sorts. If it was the left side, know that you are dealing with material considerations, which mean that there could be a job, a project, or something dealing with your sustenance that is coming to an end or is in the process of dying, which may be due to a lack of attention.

This symbol could also have a more personal association especially if you have lost someone to this event.

There are many factors to be considered. That is one of the reasons why you must expand your mind to seek to understand the messages being received.

Deer

The first thing that comes to mind is innocence, gentleness, and sustenance. Deer in a dream could also represent an annoyance, because if you live in an environment where they are always on the front lawn eating the plants or on the highway at night, then they could be a threat, a distraction and an annoyance. What is your association with deer?

Demon

Symbolic of negative aspects of Self. You have to ask in what way are you being demonic or in what way are you acting in a negative fashion toward others that they would see you as a demon.

What are the demons in your life? Is a demon approaching based on the particular cycle you are in? There are many demons: alcohol, illicit drugs, sympathy, sex, chocolate, etc.

Name your demons so that you can begin to understand how they operate in your life, knowing that it will be easier to control them and their affect on matters at hand.

Demonstrate

This depends on the type of demonstration. You could have civil demonstrations or product demonstrations. The type of demonstration witnessed in the dream or vision would depend upon the energy at work. If you are dealing with civil unrest and protesting and things of that nature, then know there is conflict at hand. There is disagreement. The anger has not culminated, but there is certainly disagreement afoot. So, there is a disharmony as energy at work.

If the demonstration is more physical and violent, then know that anger was the stronger force and communication and restraint failed.

If it is a product demonstration, then what comes into play is the type of product. Is the goal to sell you something? If so, what is it and what are they appealing to, your vanity, your convenience? What are they asking you to buy into?

Question demonstrations and if you find yourself in one in your dreams, ask yourself what is being presented and on which side of the fence do you stand? Another aspect is, if you do product demonstrations, the same questions above could also be asked by you. This puts another level of insight to work in arriving at an understanding of what this symbol means to you.

Den

If you find yourself in a den, as long as it is not one of iniquity, and even if it is, some of the following symbology applies as well. Dens denote a reading, relaxing, enjoying study within an expression environment.

Of course, there are animal dens, which would be a cave-like environment. Let us start there. If you find yourself in an animal's den or that kind of environment, it may be an indication of a tendency to withdraw and that there is something afoot that has you wanting to crawl into your cave/den and hide.

The other side of the interpretation is the protective nature of a den. It is almost the same in that it offers seclusion, but is a little bit different. Then you have a den where the library or the desk is, or it is the family room, which denotes either emotional companionship or socializing.

The office den would represent expression, work, and things of that nature. Again, it is a matter of understanding what it means to you. Was it a part of your life and what role did it play in your life? These are questions to ask of almost every symbol that arises.

The den may also serve as a place of escape. It may also be a place of entertainment and/or productivity.

Devil

The devil, or Satan, represents negative actions taken or negative aspects of Self envisioned or considered. "The devil made me do it" is a way of saying that a negative aspect of your Self, which you failed to understand or control emotionally, took you down a particular path. From a different point of view, the devil, as well as Satan both represent a lack of understanding of Self.

Diamonds

"Diamonds are a girl's best friend." Diamonds are known to be the hardest substance on earth. They are also one of the most valued substances on earth, on a financial level as well as an emotional level.

Diamonds appearing in dreams or visions would indicate opportunities for wealth, emotional gifts and emotional endowment. If the diamonds are not yours or you were not wearing them or could not get to them, then questions need to be asked; question what diamonds mean to you. Is there an opportunity for you? Who or what may be blocking you from getting one?

They would not represent poverty, but perhaps missed opportunities or a coming opportunity that may be missed if there is not more attuned matter-ological awareness.

Diesel

Diesel is a style of engine that is used in trucks, cars, buses, trains and electrical power plant generators, and all of these have their own symbology. The engine is the source of potential energy in motion.

The engine helps to drive something. Obviously, there would have to be a personal association with this.

It may well be that, as a diesel mechanic, it has one level of expression. Owning a diesel car, depending upon the type of car, may indicate a particular status one is seeking to convey. Owning a diesel truck may represent a local delivery service or a long haul freight driver, independent contractor or a trucking company.

It depends on the other aspects in the dream, vision or experience in order to get the full benefit of what is being portrayed. Keep in mind that trucks usually represent material sustenance because they carry goods and supplies, so in some way, shape or form it would be tied into material sustenance and finances.

Diesel cars would run into expression with make, model, year, etc. Diesel engines and generators may be more expressions of repairs or operators or assemblers, which would have a different connotation and different symbolic interpretation for that individual.

Digestive System

Your food (thought) is broken down into a liquid (material life) so that it can be further digested and used to nourish and rebuild the body. Of course the opposite is true of toxins in food, which will harm the body.

It is through this mental process that you evaluate the things you hear, see, and experience. You digest the situation and react accordingly, based on concepts and patterns of behavior in your subconscious mind, you will either assimilate it or reject it.

Digestive distress can come in many forms, each with its own symbolic interpretation. Overall an upset stomach indicates something being presented that is not acceptable to you on some level, therefore the conflict is manifesting as distress.

For more thorough examination of health related issues read my book, "Health and Disease Symbology Handbook," available at www.innerhealthbooks.com.

Dining Room

The dining room is traditionally formal/holiday get together place, somewhat like the kitchen. In some kitchens it is the conversation place, as well as being symbolic of sustenance or mundane or even punishment. Punishment is especially true if you are made to wash the dishes every night.

There is no telling what the association is on a personal level. Universally, it represents sustenance. The dining room also represents sustenance, but also entertainment and formal dining, formality from a different point of view.

What is your personal emotional association with this room?

Darkness

Darkness is symbolic of a lack of self confidence, which results from doubt or fear. The degree of darkness is dependent upon the degree of doubt at work in your life at that given moment based on the situation at hand.

Maybe you are working on something that is work related and you find yourself engulfed in a very dark fog. This is your mind's way of revealing your subconscious feelings. With that knowledge you can go within and seek out the concept behind those feelings. Once understood, its power over you diminishes greatly.

If the doubt is overwhelming then you could say that a person was caught up in fear. Whenever you go into a situation without insights or understandings, the situation appears to be greater than it really is. Doubt becomes the perception that is used to view the situation, and, because of that incorrect perception, certain actions or inactions are taken. These create other reactions that often lead to incompletion or failure.

Dirt

This substance can represent a lot of different energies at work. Sustenance comes to mind because of gardening and growing fruits and vegetables. If you are a builder or contractor, it could be an expression of landscaping.

You have to see where dirt has played a role in your life. If it has not and is just dirt, then you can say it indicates being grounded or if it is barren dirt where nothing is growing you may be headed into a situation of fruitlessness.

Disease

The state of health, like symptoms, conditions and diseases are the physical manifestations of the subconscious conflict between the material self and spiritual self. It is the result of conflict in your subconscious mind between who you think you should be and who you want to be.

Each disease and mishap to or in the body is fully covered in depth in "Health and Disease Symbology Handbook," available at www.innerhealthbooks.com.

Dishwasher

When this device breaks or malfunctions it may indicate that there is a difficulty in cleansing something, dealing with material sustenance.

There is always the possibility that you earn a living selling, repairing or dishwashing. In those cases you need to examine what could be interfering with your ability to earn a living. What energies are at work that will create, or have the potential to create havoc in your immediate life?

Dogs

Dogs universally represent companionship. After all, the common expression for a dog is that they are "man's best friend". However, if you have ever been attacked by a dog that universal symbolic definition is no longer valid. You will end up assigning a different symbolic significance, like fear or aggression to that type and color of dog.

In the future, when you see that dog, it will be a symbol to you that you are operating out of fear or that fear is at work in your life in whatever you are doing at the time.

Dogs, like cats, can also represent responsibility or co-dependency.

Different breeds have different symbologies for the individual. But, basically, a dog represents companionship. It can also represent obligation, responsibility.

Doors

Doors are closures or portals. They can be the opening of an opportunity, the beginning of a new cycle, or an ending, being closed off from an opportunity.

It could also be a deterrent.

If you have ever been locked in a closet or had someone jump out from behind a door and scare you, it may represent unexpected danger, terror, or fear.

Dragonfly

Dragonflies serve a purpose. They eat mosquitoes. They are also food for fish. Symbolically they can represent opportunities to rid one self of petty annoyances.

I lived by a lake and watched the fish leap out of the water to catch the dragonflies when they came down to drink. This is a symbol unto itself.

No matter how lofty you think you are and no matter what heights you think you can attain, there is always someone or something, from within the Self as well as from without, that is ready to pull you down.

Drains

They provide a way of getting rid of something. When a drain becomes clogged or plugged, what is it that is backing up on you? What is it that you cannot wash or flush down? Look around and see what exactly is going on.

Also consider whether or not there is something or some-one draining you of energy, resources, enthusiasm, etc. Look around and question everything.

Drinks

Drinks could be symbolic of pleasure, health, escape, or social-izing. You have to look at the type of drink and how it fits into your life.

Whatever way they do will give you an indication of an aspect of what is going on from a cyclical perspective. You also have to look at what is going on when this particular type of drinking occurs. What has been the motive for doing it? What was going on in your life at the time?

Symbols will help you look back in order to show you where you are so that you can see ahead and make the necessary changes.

Ducks

Ducks are interesting birds from the point of view that they are both airborne and are at home in the water, the material plane. You could feed yourselves from the material and soar with your thoughts in the spiritual.

However if the duck were to attack you, then I would say you have to look at it from a different perspective and that there are attacks coming to you from lofty thoughts.

Dungeon

When you find yourself in a dungeon, it usually denotes being a victim. It could also denote being the person who is in charge of the dungeon and inflicting pain and torture upon other people.

If you are the victim, look around and see what is going on in your life that makes you feel that you are being imprisoned and persecuted. If you are the dungeon keeper, see what is making you feel that you have control over someone and using it in a negative fashion.

More often than not, you will find that symbols will be guidance to you about what you are currently manifesting and what you have set in motion based on the particular pattern of behavior that you are in.

Remember that whatever the pattern is, it has a predetermined conclusion unless you change it, and the only way to change it is by seeing where you are in the cycle and acting appropriately by changing an attitude or initiating an action. That is what symbols tell you, so that is what such a "dungeon" may be able to tell you.

E

Earth

Earth represents sustenance, nature, and Mother Earth. There are many different ways to look at Earth. One could say it is dirt and implies poverty. Another will say it is sustenance. You could have a garden. It could be a livelihood, as in being a farmer or landscaper. This is one where you have to search your Self to see if there is a unique relationship to exactly what you are seeing in the dream to get the full benefit of the symbology involved.

Earthquake

Unstable foundations: what is going on that would cause you to lose your balance and have everything you have built come tumbling down? If you find yourself in an earthquake, look around and see what is going on in your life that could cause a quake of sorts.

Ears

Ears are your antennae. They discern, hear, and feel the thoughts, vibrations, and sounds coming at you moment by moment. These stimuli trigger subconscious reactions that are designed to fulfill expectations of self.

The ears also allow us to hear everything in relation to other people, places, and situations. They provide the ability to hear the subtleties in conversations and the concepts that are presented in life, and the truth or falsehood of ideas presented to you, and whether to accept or decline those thoughts. Some thoughts or concepts can cause you to have an unbalanced approach to things.

Elbows

See Ankles.

Electrons

Electrons are particles of an atom that exist in the outer rings and are generally known to seek balance with the protons that reside in the nucleus of an atom. The electrons have a negative charge, while the protons have a positive charge.

The questions come up: In what way were electrons in your dreams/visions? What could possibly be seeking a negative result from a particular transaction, and what might that transaction be? Remember, because dreams are precognitive, there may be other symbols in the dream to help you understand what pattern you are in; dreams are also retro-cognitive in terms of looking back in order to ensure that the pattern unfolds according to plan.

However, it is in your best interest to change that plan. Therefore, looking at everything and understanding what is going on is in your best interest. Electrons could be a negative force that is circulating around you and seeking an opportunity. Look at everything that is going on.

Elements

The word "elements" brings many different definitions to mind; from heating elements to the elements that make up the universe. Another way to think about elements is as a fundamental substance, such as water, air, fire and earth. What bearing do they have on what you are going through and what associations do you have with them?

Depending upon what the element is and how it shows up in your dreams or visions, or how you pay attention to it in life, will determine what is going on in the sense that you have an association with whatever the element is that you are looking at.

Endocrine System

This system is composed of many different glands. Overall this system is responsible for regulating the body. This is why each gland has its own symbology. Here are quick and brief descriptions. For a greater understanding of their symbology and function, read my book, "Health and Disease Symbology Handbook," available at www.innerhealthbooks.com.

Pituitary Gland: Growth, Expression
Thyroid Gland: Growth, Balance
Parathyroid: Balance
Adrenals: Courage, Strength, Inspiration
Pineal Gland: the Third Eye
Thymus: Immortality, Defenses
Pancreas: Digestive Abilities, Converter
Prostate: Aid in Reproductive Process, Control
Skin: Sensitivity, Protection, Cleansing
Reproductive Organs: Expression
Ovaries and Testes: Expression, Self-Image

Energy

When you experience low energy, you need to think symbolically along the lines of the uninspired.

When you are inspired in life, you have all the energy you need to go out and "do battle" with the forces of the material plane. These forces are both within you (your concepts and their patterns of behavior and the thoughts and belief system that are generated from same) and without (your family, your work, living environment, hobbies, etc.).

Engine

Engines are symbolic of a few different things, be it power, movement or electricity. It could be personal expression, because an engine is something that produces power. What is it that you use to produce power? In what way is your engine malfunctioning and should that be a consideration? What kind of fuel do you give your engine? From another point of view, your body is your engine. What is happening with your body?

Is the engine in your dream for driving something such as a car, truck, bus, train or plane? If so what is your association with any of those vehicles? Engines can be used to turn a generator so that it will produce electricity. Do you need a spark to get you moving? Do you need to put fuel in the tank to feed your engine so that it will run?

Entryway/ Foyer/ Vestibule

All of these signify the initial entry into whatever the symbology of the home is for the individual, whether it is security, sustenance, imprisonment, responsibility, obligation, etc.

Entryways serve different purposes in different environments. In the northern states it is a buffer to keep the cold out, it is also a place for changing, shedding winter clothing and leaving all the muddy boots in that area.

It may be a place of acclimation as well. An automatic adjustment takes place as you step into this environment that may not be as warm as the home, but is not as cold as the outside; there is a transition that takes place in this environment.

What are you going through that an adjustment is necessary? In what way are you trying to change or adapt to a new environment and how does that feel to you?

Exits

Exits are ways out. Depending upon where the exit is and what you are involved in and what you want to get out of, you could also say that exits are doorways into another environment, arena or dimension. Was the exit on the left or right side? Left would be material considerations and the right would reflect spiritual.

Eyes

In Mexico they have the superstition of the "evil eye." If you stare at a child, you have to touch that child so you do not leave the "bad eye" on them.

With regard to the eyes, look at them from the perspective of perception, vision, judgment, observation, or perhaps even people spying on you. If there are sets of eyes in dreams or visions, it could be that you may feel under the gun from more than one avenue, more than one person, more than one circumstance.

Because you use your eyes to examine things clearly, this is yet another avenue. Maybe there is a need to examine something that you are involved in to gain greater clarity. Think every way you can of perception, within and without.

Another thing that you do with your perceptions depends on your orientation at the time. Were you raised in a household where there is always a "looking" to find fault with another human being? When this happens the children may train their perceptions to see faults. You can always find the fault in another. It is very difficult to see your own faults and shortcomings.

You can train your perception to seek out opportunities. In this scenario you begin to see things from that perspective. "What is the opportunity here? What is the opening?" Be aware that there are always those opportunities, as well as probabilities; not to mention potentialities.

You also use your vision to be able to criticize, to make value judgments. You rarely use it to make a clean, clear observation. An observation is a statement of reality without prejudice, without judgment and without evaluation. This is something that is very difficult to do. You must train yourself to be able to function that way. In order to do that you really have to be in control and not emotionally connected to whatever it is you are observing or are involved in.

F

Fabric

Fabrics have multiple uses. The first application might be to protect yourself, because if you are nude you are going to take fabric and wrap it around your body to protect your nakedness from the elements.

You may use a fabric to beautify your environment or to camouflage it. You can use a fabric to make a statement of identity, such as a flag or banner. A banner may be associated with a political party. A prime example is the banners flown by the crusaders as they went from country to country. Another use would be for the announcement of a celebration or a sale.

Fabric may be an aspect of your expression if you are a seamstress or tailor.

Face

Your face is the image that you present to the world. It is a reflection of your concepts and how you see yourself. On some levels it is also how you expect others to see you.

When there is a disruption of any type on the face it indicates that you are under stress and feeling insecure in relation to what is going on in your life.

Falling

Falling in dreams could indicate that you have nothing to stand on and nothing to support you, that you are isolated and alone. What are you involved in that isolates you without external support that you feel you need? Keep in mind that you are never placed in a situation that you cannot master.

Fan

The main purpose of a fan is to provide relief and comfort in a hot, humid and somewhat stifling environment. This device is used for cooling. It creates a breeze and this cools the body down. You could examine the concepts of hot, humid and somewhat stifling environments on many different levels. After all, there are a lot of things that could get you "heated up." As a result, there may be a need to cool down.

Fans are also sea plants. If this is what you are seeing in your dreams the question becomes in what way this relates to you.

Fans can also be used as a disguise of sorts such as those used by striptease artists.

Father

This symbol can represent many different things. Fathers represent an aspect of manhood. Your father could be a person of authority. He could also be someone who is soft, gentle and loving or someone who is inconsiderate, imposing and controlling.

Of course, in some religions he is the pastor, minister or priest providing a sense of security and connection to God.

Fax Machine

Fax machines are part of communication and expression. Whether business or personal, it still pertains to communication; or there may be a personal issue with a fax machine in the sense that you may repair them or design them. You may spend your day faxing, which may just be an aspect of how you earn a living and not your expression, but it is still a communication and expression device.

Feathers

Feathers represent protection for the body of a bird. Feathers could also be an irritant or a tickler (which could also be an irritation). They could indicate being airborne, as in "light as a feather."

Again, this is an issue that requires your personal association to discover its symbology as it applies to you and your situation.

As with all symbols, you have to stretch your mind, which is the beauty of it when you see how the guidance is working for you and how you can make it work for you.

Feet

Guided by your mind, your feet take you where you want to go. You choose the direction, path or goal and then proceed. The feet represent your direction. Trouble here indicates a doubt or problem with the direction that you have chosen.

Female

The female aspect of the self is the inner connection that allows for the insights, perceptions, and the intuitive "knowing" that you need to make decisions and choices on a daily basis. It enables you to be receptive about everyone and everything around you. It also is that part of you that draws from the Creative Continuum called God.

Ferris wheel

Ferris wheels are carnival attractions and generally for amusement. They do offer a perspective when you are at the top. You can see further, so it increases your vantage point.

However, there is no forward movement when you ride a Ferris wheel. You keep going around and around. Do you feel that is what is currently happening in your life?

You may have had some wonderful times on a Ferris wheel and it brings back emotional memories of family, or a first kiss.

This is one of those situations where your personal emotional association is more important. You may have had a job in a carnival working a Ferris wheel. You need to seek to understand what it is saying to you.

Fever

A fever indicates anger. The anger can stem from resentment, frustration, guilt, or disappointment: forces that can "burn you up."

What is the source of your emotional turmoil, and why does this situation or person trigger such a response?

Fighting

Fighting is obvious in the sense that it represents conflict. If you are witnessing a fight, then you have to know that the energy of conflict, either physical or verbal, is afoot.

If you are involved in it yourself, it indicates that there is obviously anger present within and it is seeking an outlet. It also demonstrates that there was a misunderstanding of the particular pattern of behavior you are in that would lead you into an anger-producing situation that would result in fighting.

Normally, whenever there is that kind of a release of anger, resentment or frustration in a fight, it is not necessarily directed toward the person(s) with whom the fight is taking place. They are just a triggering device.

However, even then, symbology is involved with respect to the type of person it is, whether it is male or female, young or old, because everything has a symbolic value. Everything and everyone is energy at a particular vibration and, therefore, has a symbolic association to you.

Fighting can also represent internal conflict between your material Self and your spiritual Self. So, it is fundamentally an energy conflict that you must be mindful of.

Figurines

Figurines are items people buy and display around the house. On one level they are just material objects. However, they do have a representative energy so you have to think about what the figurine depicts.

Is it a thing, person or an animal? Examining this symbolically in the sense of what it does and what purpose it has will help give you some understanding. The other way to look at a figurine is to question when you bought it, what was going on in your life at the time of the purchase and why are you attracted to it now. When symbols occur it is your mind's way of trying to wake you up to pay attention to something.

Figs

Figs provide nourishment, sustenance and are very sweet. They are one of the most alkalizing fruits known. This is important because when the body is alkaline "germs" and cancer do not flourish.

There is a story about figs in the New Testament where Jesus destroyed the fig tree because it did not provide him with sustenance. Why did he do that? What is the lesson to be learned? Perhaps the lesson is that when something is of no value, let it go and do not bother with it again if it is not going to give you what you need.

You could take that in terms of helping, aiding, assisting, inspiring, encouraging. But, if it does nothing for what you need, then you do not need it, you do not need to be distracted by it, you do not need to be involved with it and you do not need to give it one iota of thought.

Fingers

Each finger has its own meaning as an indicator:

The thumb relates to control and will power. Without the use of the thumb, you could not fully control or grasp items.

The index finger relates to the emotions. Used to point and place blame.

The middle finger relates to spiritual or material aspirations. That is why it is the longest finger on your hand.

The ring finger relates to social relationships. It is upon this finger that many of your social statements are made. These are based on customs such as marriage, friendship, school rings, etc.

The little finger relates to the ego, which is of little use to us. You do not use the little finger, and the loss of it would not hamper your ability to handle a situation

Fire

This element is symbolic of the emotions. When you have a discussion with anybody about religion, you bring about emotional stimulation, which could lead to emotional conflict.

Fires consume and destroy. What is going on what is it consuming? Why is it burning you up? Who is creating situations that are heating up or where you stand to get burned?

Fire is also used for cooking. It facilitates your ability to consume and, therefore, it is associated with sustenance in an indirect way.

Fireplace

Fireplaces have many different connotations. Comfort, light, warmth and heat are one set of symbolic applications. Another possibility is that the association may be with pain, the result of being burned by embers or a hot piece of metal from a fireplace.

It could have emotional or sensual feelings. You have to question what your association with a fireplace is. Universally, I would say heat and comfort, almost external protection from the elements.

A fireplace, like fire can also relate to the emotions. Something is burning you up. Something that could be all consuming and certainly something dangerous may be in the making.

Fireworks

Fireworks bring to mind a lightshow more than anything else. From that perspective you can say that they represent a celebration. Fourth of July is a great example. In that context, fireworks may indicate a desire for a celebration, something on the horizon worth celebrating or past celebrations to be remembered.

Looking back is part of a Universal Teaching for two reasons. You look back in order to see ahead. In this scenario your mind draws on your past performance on how you handled a particular situation based on your pattern of behavior. You also look back to draw on past strengths and successes.

In what way is a celebratory energy at work in your life? There are other sides to fireworks. If someone was denied participating in or attending a fireworks show, or could not see a Fourth of July fireworks display, or was injured by fireworks, all of those would denote another aspect of the symbology of fireworks.

Fish

These creatures are symbolic of material thoughts because water is symbolic of your material life. Another symbolic representation of fish is the Christian movement or the Christian philosophy.

Fish are also symbolic of spiritual thoughts in the material plane. Different kinds of fish would indicate the different kinds of thoughts. One example is a shark. This would make you think in terms of something predatory. A barracuda would make you think of something aggressive, sleek, thin, and conniving. Salmon is something that jumps upstream against the current and is habitual and heavily pattern-influenced.

You can see that fish have individual meanings. The question is: What kind of fish are in your dreams? What is the action that is taking place? How does that relate to you on a personal level and how does it relate to what is going on at the moment?

You could have a fish story, as in your very first trout that you caught when you went fishing with your dad, brother, uncle, cousin or friends. You went fishing with your dad and that is how you learned how to fish. All different considerations are involved.

Fog

This phenomenon is the result of two different aspects converging. On one side you have hot and humid air colliding with dense cold air. The product is fog. Fog creates an inability to see clearly for any distance ahead. You are limited in your perception. You cannot look into the future. This can create pressure and doubt which can be reflected in a lack of faith.

A fog represents doubt and uncertainty about where you are going because you cannot see where you are headed. You have an idea, but there is no clear path or plan of action. This could lead to a difficulty because if you are going too fast and you cannot see, you could wreck your vehicle (of expression).

Slow down and try to change your perception from regular lights to yellow lights (caution) so you can see through the fog, the mist, through the illusion and distractions and try to get to the core of what is going on.

Food

Countless books have been written on food, but none of them address the fact that each and every item of food has a symbolic significance, and some have a special significance on a very deep emotional level for certain individuals.

When it comes to food in your dreams, you would have to question long and hard. If you are allergic to a particular food, then the questioning has to go back to when you first became allergic to this food and what was going on in your life at the time. An example of this would be a child who developed an allergy to mashed potatoes. How did that happen?

The parents may have been having an argument and one of them picked up the ladle full of mashed potatoes and threw it at the other. Some of the potatoes hit the child and that gave the child a negative association with the mashed potatoes. At this point in time, that child, who is now an adult, is allergic to mashed potatoes because it triggers an uncomfortable experience.

Try and make a list of your favorite foods. See which give what type of comfort. Try changing your diet. Try eliminating your favorite foods and see what you experience and then question why. What did that particular food represent for you?

Foyer

See Entryway.

Fruits

Fruits are symbolic of expression in the sense that they are the fruits of your labor. There is always the personal emotional association, and there are some generalizations about fruit, such as the apple being the fruit of knowledge. But, those are immaterial compared to your personal association with a particular fruit.

Fruits represent sustenance. They can be bitter or sweet, they can be easy or difficult to reach. You have to see how it would apply to whatever is currently going on and project ahead a little to see whether or not the fruits are going to be easy or difficult to reach. Whether they are fresh or spoiled is another vantage point from which to examine the fruits of your labors.

Fuel

Fuel can be made from many different substances. It can be from a liquid, such as oil, or a solid, like coal. Fuel is used for running engines that may generate power or a vehicle. Fuel can also be used in a furnace to generate heat.

Fuel is symbolic of having the resources to move forward

or supply energy to a situation. With gasoline and oil prices, it could also represent depletion.

What do you require in the way of fuel, aside from physical sustenance? What gives you the fuel to do what you do? And what type of fuel do you require to do what you want to do?

Future

The future is a glimpse of potential realities. It is something that is unsaid and something that you are constantly co-creating. Depending upon the future that you want, you must envision that future and taste it, smell it and embrace it. Then think about what would stop you from achieving it. That is where your energies need to be directed.

Futures unfold for people based on their subconscious concepts and the patterns of behavior that are created. People live to fulfill their subconscious expectations. The way to create a different future is to identify where you are in the cycle of any given pattern of behavior and change the attitude so that the outcome will be different than what usually occurs when this particular pattern is working.

Furnace

The furnace may represent heat and warmth. It could also represent work. It is something that needs to be fed in order to generate heat. You could say that there is an upcoming situation that is going to require more energy in order to generate the heat that you need for whatever the project may be, because heat can denote energy and energy expense.

If you are a repairman who works on furnaces then it would relate to your expression.

G

Garage

It is important to notice if it is enclosed as part of the house, and if the car is in the garage. When a car is parked inside the garage it indicates that the vehicle is not moving, that there is something hindering expression.

When an individual in a dream sequence finds himself or herself in the garage looking for a vehicle, looking for a way to express their self, they are experiencing feelings of being unable to find expression. See also Vehicles of Expression.

The garage could also be a place of creativity, with a workbench or a place to repair the vehicles. It also signifies the mundane, such as the washer and dryer.

Garden

This could represent expression, sustenance, joy, or labor. One would have to think about what the garden contains. Is it a flower garden or vegetable garden? Is it shrubs or trees? What does a garden mean to you?

A garden could also represent fertility, because from gardens you bring forth life. This is more of a hands-on situation and really gets into being at one with the earth. See also Vehicles of Expression.

Garden of Eden

If you find yourself in the Garden of Eden in one of your dreams, then you are in your subconscious mind and looking for that place of innocence, that place of all-knowing, of paradise prior to partaking of the material plane.

Eve eating the apple is symbolic of man's entry into the material plane. Mankind decided that the way for the soul to progress through this material dimension to be in harmony with the Creative Continuum called God was to partake of it to manipulate the lines of power that are the subtle construct of this dimension.

Mankind thought that the best way was to enter into this plane and manipulate the lines of power from the inside versus the outside. Unfortunately, mankind has lost its way. He is a prisoner in the material plane, distracted by its beauty and never seeing the truth.

Jesus was educated to see the truth, and the purpose of his life was to teach man how to master the material plane. He demonstrated it by living the Universal Teachings and truly demonstrating mind over matter, including the point of resurrecting his own body and rematerializing it.

Gas

Gas could represent a few different things because there are different interpretations to the word "gas." As a fuel, it is something that participates in sustenance, something that generates heat, energy or is employed for forward movement.

It could be something you sell or buy for yourself or a corporation. There is gas that lights and warms the house, so this brings you back to heat and sustenance in a different way.

Are you running out of gas? Do you have the fuel you need to do whatever it is that you are working on? Is there enough fuel to move you forward?

You could also perceive gas as flatulence, which generally has a vile or uncomfortable aroma. The questions that arise are:

What would be stinking up the situation? The reason I go in that direction as well is because in dreams you can smell and taste things, because although you are in another reality, it is still something energetically that you can bring back with you in order to help you understand. It depends how your mind communicates with you.

Gems

Gems are a study unto themselves. They need to be studied in-depth to understand their symbolic significance. In the Bible, there are twelve stones or gems that were used in the breastplates and aprons of Aaron and his sons before they could enter into the Holy Temple where the Ark of the Covenant was kept.

On a superficial level, gems have appeal, charm and value. Depending upon which gem is in the dream or vision that captures your attention; you need to seek to understand what your personal association with that gem is because that will be the dominant interpretation. If you cannot think of one, then just think of the value of whatever the gem is and what other relationships it may have.

Within the gem family there are amethysts and diamonds, which are referred to as "a girl's best friend." Diamonds also represent hardness and value, as well. They represent glitter, distraction and love.

There are so many different ways to look at diamonds that, again, you must go back to your own personal emotional association with it, which will be the truest definition for you to work with in any given situation.

Emeralds are known for their value and beauty, as well. They are green in color and green symbolizes healing. Jade is another precious stone. Also see colors.

Geyser

Geysers occur when water is pushed out of the ground under pressure. Water represents our material life. If there are geysers in your dream, what pressure could be building and how is it that you explode? There is a situation of a material nature brewing, so look around to see what that might be.

Glass

Glass is an interesting substance in the sense that it can be crystal clear and you can see through it, or opaque, in which case it is difficult to see through. In this case, perception is clouded and uncertain. Depending upon how the glass is used and the room it may be in, assuming you are in a room, would contribute to its symbology.

It could be a container, or it could be a windowpane, windshield, or window in a door. It depends on everything else that is present in the dream or vision, as always.

In all dreams you must look at each individual symbol as if it were a letter. Then you spell out the entire communication being presented to you.

Glass could also act as a protection or an impediment in the sense that if there was broken glass, then it may impede your forward movement for fear of being cut or having your tires deflated.

Glitter

Glitter is symbolic of distraction, because it captures the eye and the attention. It dresses something up to look nice that may not be so underneath. It requires questioning as to what or who is covered in glitter, and when glitter was a part of your life.

This substance can also lead to disillusionment because it presents a false façade.

Gold

Symbolically, gold represents thought, and the purity of thought. Gold can also represent love of the material plane. It offers a sense of security. In truth, it is a false security. The only true security is in knowing that you can master any situation you are confronted with.

It also represents power, and power can come in many different ways.

Gold is also a means of barter, a means of expression. It may also provide power. People feel powerful if they have gold protecting them. If you hide behind your gold power, that is a kind of material power, not a true spiritual power.

Grass

Grass could represent obligation, a chore, confinement, or wealth. It may also be a part of your expression on different levels. You could have a landscape business or you could grow grass for commercial sale. In what way do you relate to this type of grass?

Then you have the other kind of grass, which could represent escape, relaxation, or therapeutic use. You could have associations with different levels of interpretation. In all matters it always comes back to your personal emotional association.

Gray

See Colors.

Gray fog

Fog obscures vision. It is very difficult to see clearly through a fog. In fact, it takes a yellow light to see through it. When you look at yellow symbolically you see inspiration and insight.

When you are in a fog you may not be able to discern distance, therefore you do not know if a negative or detrimental force is approaching, how close it is and from what angle. There are all kinds of questions there that need to be asked. What are you currently involved in that you feel you cannot see clearly?

The fact that it is gray in color implies that there is some degree of doubt in your faith. It is not black and it is not white. It is a mixture of the two. What is going on and what is it that you are having difficulty looking at and seeing clearly?

Grease

A lubricant; which means there may be something going on that needs a little grease to make it go smoother. Grease will make things slippery, so there may be something you are trying to hold onto and you cannot.

Green

See Colors.

Grit/Grime

When you think in terms of something being gritty or grimy, it is mostly dirt mixed with oil. In these situations, the first thing that comes to mind is a specific attitude. If you find yourself in a gritty or grimy situation, it is like a dirty deal where you are either going to have to work very hard at it to get through it, or there are some aspects of it that are questionable.

You can also become grimy from doing dirty work or mechanical/engine work.

Guest bedroom

If you find yourself in the guest bedroom, there are a couple of ways to look at it. You could go back to the fundamental symbology of a bedroom to help on one level. However, the concept of a guest is someone who is either invited or one who is uninvited and shows up unexpectedly, or is an intrusion or an imposition.

It depends on how you feel about guest, as well as whom the guest might be in the episode. Remember, everyone who shows up in a dream is an aspect of your Self. So, even from the guest bedroom point of view, there is an aspect of your Self that you may not be familiar with that is requiring some sort of sustenance, housing or feelings of security in the subconscious mind. Keep in mind that a guest bedroom is a temporary form of housing, security. In what way do you feel that your security is temporary? In what way and in what situation are you a guest?

It is daunting to try to understand what part of you is the guest and which is the resident. You must always seek to understand and always ask, "Why? Who? What does this mean to me? How does it function?" Then all of these things will give you insights as to what you are dealing with.

Gym

This environment represents physical fitness, working out, wanting to be healthy and looking good, wanting to stay in shape. It could be part of expression if you work as a trainer or are a bodybuilder, so it could be a place of competition, training and discipline programs, or a specific approach to things.

A gym set, depending upon what it is compose of, could either be a children's gym set, which would be an immature approach to whatever it is you are trying to build or accomplish, or a home gym set, which would go back to the original concept.

Gym set

Depending upon what it is, a gym set will denote the level of maturity. It could be a jungle gym set, a backyard swing set, or a barbell or an all-in-one set that does everything.

It depends on what it is and what it represents to you and whether or not you are using one, have used one, have not used one, or hurt yourself using one.

You can see all of the different ways in which anything and everything needs to be looked at and analyzed.

H

Hair

Hair is part of Self-image. The image that hair provides plays a major part in your acceptance factor; how you see yourself and how others see you.

Hair is also symbolic of strength. The story of Samson in the Bible is the symbolic lesson.

Is your hair dry or oily? Does it have sheen or does it lack luster? Is it curly or straight? Are you always neat or do you need a trim or haircut? All of these subtle differences add depth to your understanding.

Hairpins

These are usually used to place the hair in certain patterns by restraining or letting loose, all in the name of creating a fashion statement. Some hairpins are ornate while others you can barely detect their presence and use.

Hairpins could be phallic symbols because they are long, pointed needles. If the only association a person has to hairpins is that they were once stuck by one, then you may question that there is a sticky situation coming up in which you will get stuck.

In what way were hairpins displayed or viewed in your dream or vision?

Hallway

Generally, a hallway is a passageway, a transition that allows you to go from one room or place within a building to another place within the same building. Some hallways are small, narrow or short. Others are long and wide with high ceilings.

In addition to it being a passageway, it could be a waiting area. It could be a place of exclusion, "Wait in the hallway while we take care of business."

You have to question if there is a personal emotional association with it, and where hallways dominate in your life and if there is anything emotional that took place in a hallway.

If something occurs in the hallway, then you need to question which room you were leaving and which room you were going to, and consider what you were thinking during that transition.

Hands

Your hands, along with your fingers, give you the opportunity to get a firm grip on things. Therefore, they have taken on the symbolic significance of handling and your ability to handle situations. Hands are also symbolic of self-expression. They might be used for artistic endeavors such as writing or painting, as examples.

Hard drive

Your hard drive is tied into your expression of manhood (male/female) in the sense that if you are a writer or use a computer for work, your data is there. Your entire reality is there. If the hard drive fails, and if that is the computer you use for work, there is an upcoming issue.

There may be something going on where you are in doubt about your ability to do the job and it may cause you to lose the laptop, crash the hard drive, or something to let you know that you are in severe doubt about your abilities and there needs to be some intensive questioning as to what may be going on.

The same holds true if it is tied into your expression. Work is part of someone's expression, but it may not be everything. You could be a photographer and have 3,000 pictures on your computer. Or you could be a musician and have all the music you have created on your computer's hard drive and not backed up anywhere.

You can see that having a hard drive crash and burn in this day and age could be catastrophic and heart-wrenching on many different levels. See also Vehicle of Expression.

Handbag

Handbags, purses and clutches can be for dress or sport, a place for carrying all of your belongings, your identity, keys, opportunities, money, support and, possibly, your sustenance.

Handbags, etc. can be coordinated with your clothing; they are accessories and can be part of your outfit. They can be part of your expression or your job.

This is another situation where a lot of thought has to be given to your association with handbags, purses, clutches or wallets. They are all similar but with variations. Fundamentally, they represent containers of sustenance or identity.

Head

Here is where the mind dwells. All subconscious and conscious thoughts originate here. This is why the head is considered symbolic of the spiritual plane.

Faith in Self starts here. When you have issues here it represents a lack of faith in your Self with regard to upcoming situations.

Headache

Headaches indicate that the forces of doubt are at work. Keep in mind that the head is symbolic of Spirit because this is where you do your thinking and where your mind lives and God dwells. This is also reflective of your Self confidence.

Doubt works to make you feel uncertain on how to proceed or deal with a current or up-coming situation. Colds, like headaches may be approaches that a person may use for avoiding the situation. It is caused by a lack of faith in your Self.

Handkerchief or Bandana

Both could be used as a headband (See Headband). A handkerchief is also an item that can help clean up a mess.

Hands

Your hands, along with your fingers, give you the opportunity to get a firm grip on things. Having ten fingers provides you with the ability to handle everything that you touch.

Issues here indicate doubt making one believe that they do not have the ability to handle what is occurring in their life at the moment.

Headband

Headbands can be used for many things. They can act as a sweatband when you are in a gym or working outside so perspiration does not drip into your eyes. It could also hold your hair back.

It could be a sign of affiliation with a gang or a club. It could also be something you make or sell for a living. Look at it from many different angles to see how it relates to the dream and what you are going through.

Hearse

This style of vehicle represents a form of expression coming to the end of a cycle. Fundamentally, hearses are used to transport a corpse from one location to another. So one could say it represents transition from one form of expression to another.

Look around and see what could be coming to an end. Are you comfortable with that? How will that affect you? Are you working on something that could transpire? What type of transition are you experiencing?

These are the types of questions you need to ask with regard to all symbols.

Heart

The heart is symbolic of the emotions. Heart attacks are the result of emotional stress, strain, and rejection.

It is through the emotions that we respond to all stimuli. Emotions can "blind" and debilitate, whether it is love or hate. Both ends of that spectrum will cause the eyes to swell with tears, thus distorting perceptions.

As the emotional center, the pumping action gives strength and power to ideas, hopes and wishes. These are all based on emotional needs.

Hearth

See Fireplace.

Heat

Heat can denote many different things. Here are some quick associations: Warmth, security, sustenance, protection or anger. Because heat is an environmental element, you need to see what is going on.

If something is overheated, it is letting you know there is danger and there is a problem brewing. If the car's engine is overheating, or if the air conditioner stops working and the house is overheating, there are issues afoot that need to be examined because there are energies that are leading up to a heated situation that could possibly erupt into something more serious.

Heaven

Heaven is symbolic of Spirit. God dwells in Heaven. Heaven also encompasses the air you breathe. Without it you would cease to exist. Without Spirit you do not exist.

Thoughts also take place in the thinking, non-physical realm, again "Heaven." Thoughts all originate from the Universal Mind of God in Heaven.

When you think you are in Heaven in your dream, it could lead you to think that you are in a spiritual place and all is wonderful. This is a great attitude to go into the day with. However, do not overlook the possibility that Heaven could also represent an escape from addressing what is currently going on.

Heel

The heel represents support, direction and vulnerability. It is associated with direction and support because it is part of the foot. Because the concept of the Achilles Heel, it also indicates vulnerability.

Look around to see in what ways you are vulnerable. Even though you may think you are totally protected, in what ways are you exposed? There is an opening in the armor somewhere if this symbol was prominent in your vision, dream or mind.

Hermit

Hermits may represent isolation, withdrawal, and the rejection of society. They are characterized as someone who chooses to be alone, or is alone due to circumstances. Are you the hermit in your dream? In what way do you want to be left alone? What forces are at work currently that would require isolation or the feeling of the need for it?

Highchair

A chair for the immature; you have to look at the definition of a chair, which is inactivity or authority. Again, it is a personal emotional association. It could represent children or babies, immature activity.

Highway

Highways take you from place to place. It is the terrain that you would operate your vehicle of expression upon. The symbology here will relate to whether it is one, two, four or ten lanes.

Are you on a superhighway? Are you on a country road masked as a highway? Is it a toll road? There are many different considerations, but a highway, fundamentally, provides a way of getting from point A to point B.

Of course, there could be some highway stories in your life where they are a danger, a warning, or an uncomfortable place to be. Those thoughts must also be taken into consideration.

Depending upon where you were coming from and where you were going, the highway could tell you how you are viewing that path; i.e., narrow, rocky, smooth, easy, fast, congested traffic. There are all kinds of indications there providing you insight as to how energy is flowing and unfolding.

Hills/Mountains

Hills are like mountains in the sense that they are obstacles to overcome. They could impede your progress by some degree. Hills could also be a place of playing from childhood memories.

Again, you need to go to your emotional association with hills outside of the universal symbology of being obstacles and challenges.

Hinges

These are generally used to hold two connecting objects that work together and require flexibility. There may be a project going on that may require being connected to another aspect, even within the Self, to facilitate the flexibility necessary for whatever the project or situation may be.

Horse

A horse is an interesting symbol in itself because in order for a horse to be utilized effectively, it has to be broken and disciplined. Are you in need of discipline in order to accomplish a particular goal?

A horse and horseback riding could be something you have mastered, a skill you have acquired. A horse may be an animal that you take care of, something you love or something you fear, which is especially true if a horse has ever hurt you.

Horses can have many meanings depending upon your personal association with them.

Hospital

A hospital is one of those symbolic items where the personal emotional association is going to be most important. Basically, you could say a hospital is for emergency care and recuperation, or it could be a place of employment.

What is going on that would require ultimate care or care comparable to hospital care where there is constant monitoring? What is going on that you want to avoid the hospital? Hospitals could be applied to many different levels within the Self and projects that one is involved in.

Hostel

Hostels can be treated similarly to hotels, but represent a younger, immature aspect, less expensive, frugal.

Hotel

A hotel is generally a temporary shelter. If you are a traveling salesperson, it is a need and part of your business expense. It can be where you hold meetings and gatherings.

As a temporary shelter, a hotel in a dream raises the questions, "What are your seeking shelter from? What forces do you feel are getting ready to attack? Why do you feel you are away from your security? Why is your security threatened in such a way that you feel it is best to be in a temporary shelter?"

See what is going on and where you think the threats are. If you use hotels for business, see what that issue is. Hostels also fall under a similar category as hotels.

There are some who live at hotels as their residence. In this case the symbology would mirror those thoughts given to the Home.

House/Home

The house is symbolic of different things to different people. For some people it is a place of security, for others it may be a place of imprisonment, responsibility, and for others a sense of pride.

From some perspectives it is very difficult to assign a specific symbolic interpretation to an item because of the personal emotional association that an individual would have with that particular element or item.

I

Inactive

This speaks for itself and says exactly what is going on. The questions are: What is going on? Why would you become inactive?

People become inactive because of doubt or fear, which breed uncertainty. The inactivity will lead to an incompletion, which could be in keeping with the success-failure pattern[23].

Remember that symbols are precognitive, so you may be in an action cycle now, but there is something brewing that would cause you to become inactive. The question needs to be asked: How would what is going on cause me to become inactive? Whatever else it was tied to is an indication from which direction the energy of inactivity will be pushing you.

Inner Self

Your Inner Self follows a master plan, a kind of primary spiritual directive. That plan is to express the Harmony of the Creative Continuum called God through the understandings and practice of the Universal Laws, expressed as Teachings.

Insects

Insects can be annoying little things, pests. You have to question when you are under attack by insects: What are the annoying, petty things going around you and biting you, eating you up, irritating and aggravating you?

If you have insects such as ants, spiders, cockroaches and termites, to mention but a few, what is going on in your head?

It all comes down to petty annoyances. What are you open and receptive to? What are the types of things and people that annoy you?

Inside

This could represent security and warmth or it could be insecurity, imprisonment, confinement or restrictions. It also depends on what room or thing the individual is inside, which would further explain the symbology of the message or provide additional symbols so that the message could be understood and applied directly.

Instrument

An object used for sound, tone and harmony. An instrument can be many things. It could be a musical instrument, a medical, dental or surgical instrument. An instrument is a tool that may or may not be used in one's expression.

Depending upon the tool, it will give some insight. See Vehicles of Expression for further understanding of the concept of expression.

Insurance

Insurance represents a sense of security. It can come from doubt, as well as courage and strength, because if you have the capacity to provide for others, then insurance is one of those vehicles that will do it.

If insurance shows up in dreams or consciousness as something you are paying more attention to than normal, there could be security issues or protection issues that need re-evaluation to see if you are doing enough to protect whatever it is you are seeking to protect.

Intestinal tract

Absorption, protection; these are but two functions. The intestinal tract receives the food in semi-liquid (chyme) form that the stomach prepares through the enzyme and muscular process of digestion. Nutrients, as well as toxins, are broken down to molecular sizes. This is what is absorbed through the intestinal wall.

When a physical symbol is needed to get your undivided attention, the mind directs the brain to initiate the situation in the intestinal tract that will exclude a particular nutrient from being used. This in turn will create a shortage and set up the opportunity for disease. This is in keeping with your Self-image and concepts, and it is related to a current situation.

J

Jail

Jail represents confinement; unless you are a guard. You could also say that jail is a place of discipline because there are set times for everything. It is characterized by confinement and conformity. Imposition is another appropriate term.

In what ways do you feel confined, imprisoned? Think also of who or what may be limiting and hindering you. See them as less severe means of confinement, but imposition nonetheless.

Jamboree

It may be a get-together, party, escape, entertainment, or simple socializing. These are all different ways a jamboree can be interpreted. Gatherings, such as the Boy Scout or Girl Scout jamborees, are great examples of a multi-purpose event. You need to see how any of those definitions fit into what you are doing.

You can see by this that each symbol has multiple definitions. The real key to understanding is to relate it to what you are going through at the moment, and what you have gone through in the past that this particular symbol has meaning to you.

Jellyfish

This could represent aggression if a jellyfish has ever attacked you. It is an uncomfortable annoyance from something unique and different.

Jellies, Jams and Preserves

These are all in the same family, just different in terms of consistency or amount of sugar. Regardless of how you look at it, one could say that jellies, jams and preserves are a sweetening on top of the main issue.

If it is peanut butter and jelly, toast and jam, there is something that dresses up something else to give it more flavor or zest or zeal. What is it that you are going through that requires some jelly, jam or preserves or perseverance, as the case may be?

Jersey/Shirt

A shirt represents protective clothing. It could also tie into image. The symbology will also depend upon whether it has long sleeves or short sleeves as well as the type of shirt, whether it is a dress shirt, casual shirt, T-shirt.

Depending upon how it is viewed may relate to what is going on or what kind of a social function one may be involved in or need to dress for.

Jet Plane

A vehicle of expression. As a passenger, you are at the mercy of the pilot. You are subject to the concepts of whoever is in the pilot's seat. See also Vehicles of Expression.

How does a jet plane fit into your dream, as well as your life? What is currently going on that you would want or need a flight to, or away from, someplace or someone? What is going on that makes you feel that way?

Jewelry

Jewelry is an extension of Self and is part of the imagery one seeks to present. "Look at me, look at what I have, and look at what I own."

It could be part of expression if you design jewelry or are a craft person who makes jewelry. It could be a way of trying to accumulate wealth or material possessions, again saying, "This is what I've achieved. This is what I've accumulated."

There is always the possibility that the piece of jewelry in your dream is one with which you have a personal emotional association.

Jewish/Judaism

Being of the Jewish faith is like any other religion, and represents a particular belief system. What is interesting about Judaism is that if you look at it throughout the Bible, you will find that it begins with one man, Abraham, and culminates in one man, Jesus of Nazareth, who was a Jewish Rabbi/Teacher.

When you read and understand the Bible symbolically, you see that it is a handbook for spiritual development, going from an Adam-level of consciousness to achieving the Christ-level of consciousness. To achieve this state of consciousness you must understand the lessons contained within the Bible.

When you look at the journey of the Jews throughout the history of the Bible, you will see that they struggled to be free from Egyptian rule and, later, Roman rule. Egypt and Rome both represent the physical/material body, the carnal mind.

The purpose of your journey is to free yourself from the carnal mind and become one with the God-mind, Spirit-mind, and the Creative Continuum.

Jews are symbolic of spiritual thought as Spirit struggles to free itself from involvement within the material plane.

Joke

I have always felt that jokes were subtle forms of aggression against another individual, and certainly when they are at someone else's expense. Jokes at one's own expense can represent a lack of self-acceptance, putting oneself down, demeaning oneself, false humility.

How do jokes fit in your life? Do you use them as ice-breakers when in new situations or with new people?

Jousting

This was a sport, or more correctly, an expression of manhood. It represents combat and confrontation. The confrontation is conducted with long lances from horseback. The lances are long phallic symbols that are used to try to knock your opponent off a horse. A horse is symbolic of discipline.

If this is in your dream then the question is: Is someone trying to knock you off your discipline or are you trying to knock yourself off your discipline?

Why is your expression a threat, a danger, a conflict, a combative concern to someone else? Who might that be? Are you conflicted within yourself about this, that or the other?

You could also question the color of the horse, which would give you further insight into this symbolic communication. Are you wearing armor or are you vulnerable? What is the nature of your armor? These are all different types of questions that require thought and seeking answers.

Jumping

Jumping up and down may represent joy, excitement, oreven trying to jump out of the way of a situation. Maybe you need to be more cautious; more concerned, or be careful about what you are jumping into.

Maybe you jump around, and that should not be a part of your career résumé because it shows instability and, possibly, that something is going on that you need to question from that perspective, as well as the others that have been mentioned.

K

Kaleidoscope

When you look through the lens of a kaleidoscope, it shows you the same scene viewed from multiple perspectives. You are looking at one thing, yet it appears to be many.

How does that apply to the situation you are in currently? Do you have a tendency to look at things from different vantage points? Or do you see everything as being the same without differentiation?

Kangaroo

Kangaroos can jump from place to place. (See Jumping). Being marsupials, kangaroos carry their young in a pouch. What is it that you are toting around? What immature aspect of Self, or what responsibility do you have that makes you feel inhibited, encumbered, burdened or is something you have to carry about?

Karma

This word represents a concept that affects being. There is no such thing as good or bad Karma. There is just Karma, and it is simply a law of action-reaction. In truth, all of us have Karma to work out. We have, through our lack of understanding and through a lack of Self-knowledge, and nothing else, have taken actions that others may have deemed hurtful, sinful, and neglectful; whatever the case may be. These actions are what have set Karma in motion.

That, in turn, may set up concepts and possibly relationships to be worked out in this life cycle. What is not accomplished in terms of understanding is carried forth to the next life. In the Bible, "God requires that which is past." (Ecc 3:15)

That is all Karma is. It is working it out. It is part of the cleansing process, cleansing man made concepts from the subconscious mind.

Kerchief

A kerchief may be used as a head covering. (See Handkerchief and Bandana). It could have religious connotations, gang affiliations or grandmother connotations, the traditional ways of doing things.

It could be that you ride motorcycles and use it to hold down your hair, which is another application. All of these things are applicable and require thought.

Keys

Universally speaking, keys are symbolic of opportunities. A key is like an understanding. You use a key to unlock and open something. There are different kinds of keys. You could have a key to your business. In this case, the key would be involved in your material sustenance. You could have a key to unlock your computer. This could also be symbolic of locking away and protecting your knowledge. You may need a key to get into your computer to express yourself, to write a great novel.

You need a key to start your car. A car is also a symbol of the "vehicle of expression." Vehicles of expression are those activities that take you from one place to another. See also Vehicles of Expression.

You may have a key to a lock box where you have all your

money, gold, silver and jewelry stored.

A key also lets you in your house, which could be symbolic of security. It could also represent obligation and responsibility.

Keys also give you options. They are for specific things. The overall concept in regards to options is that any time you can unlock something you automatically have options. Every door takes you to some place and something and an opportunity is present.

Every path you take leads to a fork in the road. And at some point another decision has to be made as to which way you are going to proceed. Every time you question something it takes you to a decision. Every time you open a door and enter in you are confronted with a decision. Do I continue to move forward? Do I go to the right? Do I go to the left? Do I go in the back door? Do I go in the side door? All of those questions arise.

If you were in a dream and you found yourself going in and turning to the right, then you have to look at the symbology of the right. The right side represents the intuitive, the female, the spiritual and the future. The left side is the material, the aggressive, the male and the past.

Then there are the keys in music. I do not know how that symbol would come to you because a musical key is not a physical object as much as it is a perceived concept. However, looking at a key from that perspective is also very symbolic. In some cases those musical keys are even more symbolic.

Keys in music tell you the pace, the tone, the pitch, the rate, the feeling of what is going on. Keys in this scenario impart all those kinds of different insights.

Lost or Misplaced Keys

Lost keys are an indication of a doubt at work on some level. In fact, doubt affects all issues differently. In this case it is a matter of authority, expression; because by not having your keys to your vehicle means that you cannot move forward, you cannot express yourself, cannot go from place to place. This loss may also tie in with expression, sustenance, especially if you are a salesperson.

If you lose your physical keys, you have to deal with all of those symbolic aspects. You would have to look at the following considerations. What is on your key chain? Where were you when you last remember having them? Where were you headed? What were you involved in? Were you involved in a project, were you just leaving the house, did you have to go to work? What did you have to do all of a sudden that created a situation that you misplaced or lost your keys?

Regardless of the answers, which will give you important insights, you were being affected by doubt and fear. This is because there was an issue that you could not find your ability to unlock the knowledge that you needed in order to move forward. Keys represent opportunities and your ability to unlock situations and guidance in terms of how to move forward.

Keys also tie into security, especially if you are locked out of your house. Keys are a form of authority because they give you the ability to open doors. Losing keys can represent missed opportunities.

Kicking

If you are kicked, or if you are kicking someone in a dream, you would think in terms of aggression, disharmony, or that something is going wrong. In what ways would you like to kick the habit, kick the bucket, kick the ball, or kick the person?

You have to look at it from as many different angles as you can in order to get the benefit of this particular symbolic demonstration of an action. Fundamentally, this is aggression.

It could also be expression if you kick a ball and you play soccer or football and this is a major source of entertainment for you, a major source of expression. It could be a diversion, a distraction; it could be where your money is going.

Kickstand

This is used to support bicycles and motorcycles when they are not in use. In what way are you looking to put your vehicle of expression at rest?

The times that you use a kickstand is when you are not operating the vehicle. What type of a vehicle do you have; a motorcycle or a bicycle? What is going on that would make you think of less involvement or less activity?

Kidneys

The kidneys remove toxins and waste from your bloodstream. They help to balance the water levels in the body, as well as the acidity and alkalinity of the blood stream.

Kidney problems can mean an imbalance in life. Some concept about material life is not being understood and eliminated from the mind. This means that a person is maintaining concepts that are polluting the body/life. There are two types of cleansing, the physical, and the more important emotional/spiritual.

Spiritual cleansing is the process of eliminating man-made ideas, values and standards that are based on misconceptions and misinterpretations of the truth. When the kidneys malfunction, the place to look within is in the inability to cleanse misconceptions from the subconscious mind.

Killer Whale

Whales are mammals that live in the ocean, which tells you that there are some mighty thoughts that dwell within the material plane. It could be that there is a big thought or a big project you are working on and it may be that you need to understand the habits of a killer whale so that they may be applied where appropriate.

All animals have a lesson for us, but in order to understand the lessons you have to understand the habits of the animal, including where it lives (caves, fields, mountains etc.) and how it hunts.

Kindergarten

A school level for children; it is a symbol that implies immaturity. There is also an educational aspect. If you are a teacher, then it is a vehicle of expression.

There may be some association with it being the hardest time of your life. You may not remember anything dealing with kindergarten, but for it to come up in a dream or as a symbol or as a memory, then there is a personal association with it and it would benefit you immensely to discover the meaning of it.

Kite

Toy. Fun. Relaxation. Flying a kite is something you perhaps did with your child or grandchild, or something you loved to do as a child. This is one of those things where the universal symbolic interpretation is one thing, but the personal emotional association will be your better guide to getting insights as to how this is applicable to whatever is going on.

Kitchen

Kitchen is symbolic of sustenance because this is where your meals are prepared and may be consumed. It could also be a gathering place where everyone sits around and chats over coffee or tea.

It could represent a social environment or a family gathering. It could also represent the mundane because this is where cooking, dish washing, and things of that nature are done.

Kittens

These represent an immature aspect of cats. (See Cat). There is also the possibility that kittens represent responsibility, not from the co-dependency point of view, but maybe your cat recently had kittens.

In this scenario they are part of expression, part of responsibility, because you just cannot take off and do things when you have a cat and kittens that you are responsible for.

Knees

See Ankles.

Knife

A knife can be an attack weapon, a defensive weapon, or it could also assist in the provision of sustenance. A knife can be used to butcher animals, or cut your meat thin, or your vegetables to a size you can easily chew and digest. A knife also represents an expression of manhood because it is somewhat phallic.

Are there events occurring that you need to cut through? Are there situations where you need to defend yourself against others by your own expression? Is someone's expression of manhood a threat to you? Look at the other symbols in your dream and think back over the last couple of days to see what has taken place.

L

Ladder

A ladder is used for climbing, for aspiring, for assistance in achieving. When this symbol appears in a dream or vision, how and where it is utilized will give additional insight and guidance.

This will give you an indication as to what it is you are trying to aspire to or overcome, in the sense of getting on top of it.

Large

There are messages written on side view mirrors that say, "Objects are closer than they may appear." Maybe if something is large it may appear to be overwhelming to you. It could also be warning you that a large force is headed your way.

Look at what you think is large, exaggerated, overstated and/or overwhelming. I use those terms because it is going to depend on the amount of working faith you have in yourself. The more doubt and fear that takes hold, the larger this force or energy looks.

Larger room: Expanse, more to learn, to see, opening up, discover the within.

This more or less speaks for itself. The question arises: What type of room is it? That is where the symbology or greater insights will be gained.

Is the room so large that you are lost in it? Do you feel comfortable in it? Do you have control over it? What is the room used for or how do you intend to use it? What do you find yourself doing within the room? How is that pertinent to what is currently taking place in your life.

Remember that you will never have a vision, dream or memory if it is not related to something that is currently going on in the here and now.

Lawn

The lawn may represent the mundane, beauty, attraction, appearance and presentation. These are all the ways that the neighbors see you from one perspective. The lawn can also represent obligation.

It could be that it is a form of expression from an earning perspective, as well as a design maintenance perspective. Also, if there are flowerbeds, this is another form of creative expression. Here you are seeking to make something beautiful out of the dirt. A garden is seeking to create sustenance from one's own efforts.

Lead

Lead (pronounced "led") is a base element. The first thing that comes to mind is shielding. If you have a lead shield, what are you trying to protect your Self from? Who are you trying to protect your Self from?

Lead is also a very heavy metal. In this regard a question may be: Do you feel weighted down with responsibility or obligation? What is weighing on your mind? What is going on that makes you feel as if you have lead in the seat of your pants?

Lead

In what ways do you need to take the lead? In what ways are you being led? What is going on that would lead you astray? Again, in all the different ways that you can think of the word "lead" and all of its different applications is the way that you need to look at it symbolically and apply it to whatever is going on in the current situation.

Lean

When I first looked at this word, it made me think of a lean-to, protection and shelter. You could lean on someone for sustenance, support, encouragement, a favor. Meat can be lean. Times can be lean. Lean denotes a lack of fullness as another symbolic interpretation.

Learn

An educational symbol; learning could be part of a process, as in going for your Bachelor's or Master's or Doctorate degree.

You might be involved in a project that you need to learn something about. How is it that you approach learning? What does learning make you think of? What do you go through when you are confronted with a situation where you have to learn?

What is going on that you can look at and learn from it? Learning deals with knowledge and expression, as well as opportunities for growth and advancement.

Leave

To leave a place, be gone. To disappear, vacate. What is it you are trying to get out of? What kind of a situation do you want to leave?

Remember that symbols are also precognitive, so they tell you what is going on in the now, but they also give you a look at what is upcoming. Are you always leaving situations or people behind? What are you currently involved in that you have a desire to leave behind? More poignantly, is there a pattern-influenced approach of leaving behind?

Left side

The left side deals with material considerations. It reflects the past and how you draw on that past in dealing with the present. The left side represents the male aspect of the self.

Legs

See Arms.

Lethargy

Lethargic: inactive or barely active, slow to move. In what ways are you being lethargic? How do you feel about lethargy? Do you partake in it? Do you think it is a terrible habit? Search your feelings and see what your attitude is, because your dream may be telling you that this attitude is at work in whatever particular relationship the lethargy was taking place.

Levy

A levy is something designed as a matter of protection; built to keep the water out and prevent flooding. When you think of water, look at the symbology, it represents the material plane.

You may have driven along a levy or were stranded on one. Possibly you helped to build a levy.

Thinking of the levy as a defense, what are you defending your Self against? In what ways are you trying to protect your Self from immersion in a material project? Why? Do you feel that something could be overwhelming, could wash you away; could cause you financial destruction or ruin? What energies are at work that you need to protect your Self from?

Lice

Cephalic irritants; distractions. Because they are in the head, they relate to spiritual or faith matters, faith in Self. The head, being symbolic of spiritual domain, anything going on there has to relate to the Self and faith in some way. It denotes discomfort in the spiritual realm.

Light

Light is symbolic of insights. Whenever you have an insight to the workings of a situation you are better prepared to deal with it. Light is also symbolic of courage and confidence, as well as truth.

Lightning

Lightning is an electrical discharge that is generated when clouds rub together. Clouds have great substance, and when the two masses of air rub together they generate energy. That energy is discharged as lightning. It may be that you love to watch lightning storms.

It may be that you have been struck by lightning or lightning started a fire. This is yet another situation where you must go back to your personal emotional association in order to get the greatest amount of clarity.

Line

The symbology here depends on the definition or the experience one is having with a line. Are you waiting in line for something? If so, what are you waiting on? Is it a line to get into someplace? If so, what are you trying to get into?

Standing and waiting in line could also denote inactivity and that there are many ahead of you seeking to do the same. So, the question is: What can you do to get yourself out of the line and to the front of the line, or bypass the line altogether?

The line could be something on the ground, as in a line to cross. It could also mean to fall in line or to get behind a line. What are you confronting that decisions have to be made? Where do you draw the line in the sand about whatever it is that is going on?

Think about the many different ways you can apply the understanding or definition of a line and see how that applies to everything that is currently going on.

Lips

Lips represent communication and imagery. If you have an injured lip that prevents you from speaking clearly, what is it that you do not want to say? What is it that you feel you will be attacked in some way if you do say it?

What if you have a fever blister? They come from stress, so where is this stress, and what is it that you are uncomfortable with? What are you going through that it affects your image and the way people see you?

Think of all the different expressions that go along with the lip. What about a "fat lip?" What does that imply to you? Do you feel threatened by someone or something?

Liquid

There are so many ways to interpret liquid. It could be a liquid of sustenance, such as juice. It could be a corrosive acid, or it could be paint.

A liquid is a fluid situation. What is going on in your life that is fluid? Another way to look at it is being in water and having a fear of drowning. What do you feel overwhelmed with? Why do you feel you are in a situation you may not be able to flow out of, swim out of, climb out of, or navigate through depending on the viscosity of the liquid?

Listening

To truly listen one must have "ears that hear." How many times have you listened to someone and could not hear a word they were saying because they had absolutely nothing to say? What is it that you need to hear from your Self and what advice is out there from others that you do need to listen to and think about and examine?

Listening is one of the defense mechanisms that can save your life. That is why it is vital that you know what you are hearing. Always seek to listen to the subtleties, because from that you will also gain more insight and understanding.

Literature

Its connotations include books, information, and education. Literature is, generally speaking, educational pieces that can have the affect of growing the mind. It could also be part of one's personal expression. This is especially true if you are a writer, illustrator, editor or publisher.

It could be a diversion if you spend all of your time reading and there is no interaction with real life. That is avoidance and living vicariously.

Also, consider the type of literature and where it was in your dream or vision. The type and location will add depth to the symbolic interpretation.

Little

This size may be small and confining. Are you in a little room, a little boat or a little car? Look at the rest of the symbology in order to get the full benefit of the opportunity for a lesson.

What is it that is of limited resources for you, or limited in its availability to you? What are you going through that you thought was small, or did not see it as being large but subconsciously you do and, therefore, you will make different assessments and different interpretations, which will ultimately have a different outcome? It is wise to question what is so small.

In what ways and in what arenas do you feel little? Is there someone who makes you feel this way? Why?

Liver

The converter, the protector, and the cleanser; the primary purpose of the liver is to convert substances into glycogen (sugar) for the body to function. It also cleanses the blood by converting toxins into harmless substances for elimination. What cannot be eliminated through the normal cleansing channels will be stored within the fat produced by the liver.

The liver secretes bile necessary to utilize fats contained within the food from the diet.

The liver is a chemical factory that converts substances into useful building material. It also works at protecting the body from harmful toxins. The mind seeks to do the very same with thoughts that are presented. Those that are in agreement with subconscious concepts are used to build whatever will reflect the internal subconscious expectations. Those that are not are eliminated.

Consider the possibility that if you are programmed with certain concepts then the body will accept only those substances that will facilitate the manifestation of the physical aspects of the particular concept at work.

In the same respect the mind through the body will block the uptake of certain nutrients, thus preventing the balance and harmony essential to avoiding the disease altogether.

Difficulties are symbolic of being overwhelmed, not being able to breakdown what is being presented as a toxic. Overindulging is another factor that should be examined to understand what is going on. Undernourishment is also a key factor, especially when you see what you are lacking nutritionally and examine it symbolically.

Living Room/Den/Family Room

The living room is where one can escape from the world physically and relax. It also serves as the family room; a place of gathering. It also can represent entertainment.

This area is a place where you disconnect from the world.

Lizards/Chameleon

Entertainment, attraction, responsibility and some are able to cling to walls and ceilings.

Depending upon the relationship that you have with the lizard - it could have been your pet or work-related - it will influence the symbology in different ways.

Lizards and chameleons have the ability to adapt and adjust to their environment, so they become invisible, per se. The question comes up as to what it is that you are going through that an aspect of yourself that is tied into your image is feeling the need to go through a chameleon-like change. Who or what are you seeking to be invisible to? Who or what are you trying to cling to; get a better hold on?

You can also look at a lizard as being reptilian. This presents another series of interpretative considerations. When you think about reptiles, you look to the expression of manhood, and when you think snake/lizard reptilian they are phallic looking. Lizards also have an elongated body, so you are dealing with a similar kind of energy. This may indicate that there may be a very subtle expression that is at work that you may end up taking it on the chin.

It is advantageous to question why you would be drawing that energy to you. What purpose does it serve?

Lose your pen

All writing instruments are part of the vehicle of personal expression. (See Vehicles of Expression). You can use the pens to write, draw and communicate. If you lose a pen, then the questions become: What is it that requires your signature, your authorization, your participation or your activity in terms of your expression? How does that relate to what you are currently going through?

Lungs

The entire respiratory system feeds your body with life-giving energies such as oxygen and nitrogen, and eliminates used and potentially harmful gaseous matter. You inhale that which will nourish and sustain you, air (spirit). You exhale that which is used and is no longer beneficial, such as man-made ideas of how to be and act. It is the reflection of faith in the Self.

Any issues in this system indicate a doubt at work, a lack of faith in your Self with regard to a current situation. Look around and question what you are going through. See how you handled it in the past? What would you change? Understand why you think you cannot change the now and the understanding will provide you with the ability to alter the pattern of behavior.

M

Maggots

Maggots are symbolic of pestilence, dirt, filth, and decay. They are fundamentally young larvae of flies, and flies are dirty and can contaminate food. They can carry germs and bacteria from place to place and can infect the body through depositing filth in cuts and sores. Maggots are used in the forensic environment to clean flesh from bones and skulls in order to get a clearer picture of what may have been the cause of death.

Decay will usually draw flies and, subsequently, maggots. What is rotting away due to a lack of attention, lack of nourishment, lack of concern?

What do you need to clear away in order to see the truth of something? These are different ways to look at things.

Males/Men

The male aspect of Self is your outward expression of who you are. It is that part you draw on when you need courage and confidence to face external situations. It is your ambition and motivation to grow and go forward in life.

As a woman having the appearance of a man in dreams, the questions become: In what way do I need to express my self, be more aggressive in my current endeavor? How do these men relate to me? Who are they? And why am I in a man's body?

When you have people in your dreams that you do not know, they are all aspects of your Self. Even those that you do recognize are also symbolic of some aspect of you.

Another aspect of males/men is that they may represent authority, suppression, dominance and control. On the other hand, however, they may be soft and easy going.

You need to examine your subconscious concepts as to what you believe men are and what you expect from them and that relationship. These statements also refer to men as well as women.

Marks

It depends if they are scuff marks, water marks, stain marks, blemishes, distractions, or imperfections. See how it applies to what you are going through and how it affects what the rest of the vision or dream is about.

Where are the marks? Are they on your skin, walls, floors, ceilings, cars? What is being scuffed up, marked up, or marked down?

Marks can also be a form of grades. It all depends on the dream. Did you get passing grades in the dream? What did the grades mean to you? Is there some authority that you need to prove yourself to; do you need to produce good results?

Matches

Matches are used for starting a fire, igniting something, illuminating something. What are you trying to light? What are you trying to start up? In terms of lighting, are you talking about cigarettes or cigars? Is a match used for pleasure or escape?

They could be used for heat and that could relate to survival. What type of matches are they, wood or paper? Are matches tied into your expression? See Vehicles of Expression.

Matter

Matter is not something you would think to say you saw in a dream or vision. Whenever you hear the word "matter" you may think of, "What is the matter?"

From another point of view, matter is part of the material plane. It is the solid manifestation of condensing energy.

Matter represents thoughts, which is why symbols are such an important language. The association that you have with the physical matter and the understanding of its symbology is where you receive your guidance.

Merry-Go-Round

Merry-Go-Rounds are like Ferris wheels; they go round and round, cycle after cycle. Being on the merry-go-round indicates two energies that are at work in your subconscious and manifesting outwardly immediately; you have been here before and you are going in circles. This is a prime example of the cliché, "History repeats itself." Your personal history, patterns, also repeats and that is why you are here again.

What particular things you are currently involved in fit that description? (See also Ferris wheel). Look at everything that is going on. Try to get a fix on where you are in a particular pattern of behavior and try to project ahead as to the usual outcome. By seeing where you are in the cycle gives you the opportunity to find a way out/off the merry-go-round.

Messages

Messages represent communication. So the question comes up: Are they messages you are sending or messages you are receiving? What is the nature of the messages? What do they relate to?

Are you trying to send someone a message and they are not getting it or understanding it? Is someone trying to communicate something to you? Is there something you need to see? Is there something you need to understand?

Meters

When you think of meters, you might think of gas, electric or water meters. Meters are devices for measuring. In what way are you being measured? In what way are you measuring something you are contemplating or involved in?

Meters are also distances. Do you feel distant from something? Are you trying to get hold of a concept or idea and feel that you are missing it and it is not within your reach?

Taxi cabs also have meters. Is your meter running? Are you adding up the cost of something that you are going to present to someone? How does this relate to what you are going through at the moment?

Mice

Mice are rodents and, as such, they represent pestilence, dirt, annoyance, threats, and poverty. On the other hand, they can be a pet, a responsibility or even an aspect tied into expression.

What does a mouse mean to you? Where did you see the mouse? Was it in a home, office, warehouse or park? Each environment has its own symbology.

In understanding the symbology here, it would be beneficial to see the context in which the mouse is seen. Once again, you need to add up all the symbols and construct an understanding out of the accumulation of the data gained from reading the symbols.

Mice also like to build their nests in dark places. Is there something brewing in dark places within your Self? Are there places that offer you nesting within your Self?

Miles

Miles are like meters in terms of measurement. The question that comes into play with this symbology is the number of miles involved, which would add more understanding to the distance that has to be traversed in order to accomplish your goal or get to where you want to go. Also, look at the symbology of the number of miles.

Milk

Milk could imply the need for comfort, sustenance, security, approval. Milk is symbolic of maternal sustenance.

In a dream, milk can also indicate the need for the mineral calcium, because calcium, being symbolic of strength, also relates to the maternal aspect in the sense that children draw strength from their mother when they feel that support.

When rejection is the form of approval then there will not be any support. This would be fine for the soul that uses rejection as a form of approval.

The type of milk would also have some bearing on the symbology. There are different types of milk; regular, 2%, non-fat, soy, almond and rice.

Mirrors

Mirrors are symbolic of reflection. Is there a mirror image? Do you need to mirror your Self? What is it that you need to see?

What reflection are you missing? What type of reflections are you presenting as opposed to your regular self?

Mission

Mission has two different connotations to it. One is being on a mission, which is your personal journey toward Self-expression and unification with God. The other is a mission like the Alamo. It is a church environment that was set up during the colonization of Texas/Mexico/California.

Missions could represent houses of worship, a historical site, or a place to visit on vacation. Because of its uniqueness, I would think that in this particular instance there might be a strong personal emotional association with this symbol.

Due to the association with the Alamo, it may be that a mission represents defenses or defending, obviously not in a very successful way from a physical/material point of view.

Mold

Mold can be deadly, which you may recall in the first Legionnaires Disease outbreak in Philadelphia in the 1980's. Mold slowly eats away at whatever it attaches to. Where it cannot eat away, it becomes a growth so that it continually expands and pollutes the environment, whether it is in an air duct or in a lung within the body.

Once mold takes hold, it is difficult to remove and requires thorough cleansing. It is not always necessarily seen, especially when there is mold in the bathroom that gets behind the silicone in showers. You have to dig it all out and treat it, then reapply the silicone. The same technique has to be applied to anywhere you think mold may be growing.

It has to be examined, torn apart, cleansed and rebuilt. Where may mold be growing in your life? What is it that you think is the mold? How is it affecting your health, your vitality, your inspiration, your desire, your motivation? What is it clinging to? What environment is it growing in?

Do you feel that there are some who are like mold that have attached themselves to you and will not let go? Who are they and why are they holding on? How is that affecting you?

Moles

A mole can be a birthmark, in which case, depending upon the size and place of the mole, it could be an indication of sensitivity in a particular area. Examine the area symbolically.

There are creatures that are moles that burrow in the ground. They are generally blind. In what way are you not seeing what you must? Are you burrowing your head in the ground, in the darkness so as not to see what you must confront and resolve?

Money

Money represents many different things to people. It can represent security, sustenance, power, authority, and/or wealth. It can also indicate deprivation if you do not have it.

There are many different symbologies for money, and this is another situation where you must question what the money means to you on a personal emotional association level, because that is the one that is going to be the most dominant and is going to require the most thought. It is also the one interpretation that will provide you with the greatest understanding so that you can move forward.

Monkey

Like all animals, monkeys represent a variety of things. Monkeys are considered to be physiologically close to humans, which in itself opens up a door for diverse kinds of thinking.

Monkey business, monkey shenanigans, acting like a monkey; there are all kinds of applications for the concept of monkey. Is there any monkey business going on? Where and with whom?

Did you ever have one as a pet? Were you ever attacked by one? Did you ever have to care for one?

Moon

The moon is symbolic of emotions. What is interesting is that the moon has no light of its own. It is strictly a reflection of the source, which is the sun.

The sun represents inspiration, spirit/God and shows you that emotions reflected in the symbology of the moon are only a reflection of the truth of the light, and when the emotions are in control then you are out of conscious control.

Was the moon shining on you, for you, because of you? Was it a full moon or a partial moon? Was it an eclipse? Was there a halo around the moon?

These are all the questions that need to be asked in regards to the moon's symbology within your specific dream or vision. The moon, being symbolic of reflecting emotions, raises the question: What is going on emotionally that you are either in doubt about requiring illumination, or are in the preparatory cycle and seeking to deal with it emotionally?

What is the source of your emotional responses? You know from this material and my other work that it is the subconscious concepts that will stimulate the reactions. So the question is: What is the nature of the source? Look at the concepts.

When you are having an emotional reaction, and your dreams and visions are telling you that you are entering into an emotional cycle, question what is going on, what emotions are stirring around. Do not lose sight of the fact that doubt and fear are two of the greatest emotional stimulators. They can induce depression and inactivity or simply the feeling of being overwhelmed. All are tied into emotions and reflections of concepts.

Mosquitoes

This insect is symbolic of petty annoyances, the little things that are biting at you and draining your sustenance.

Look around and see what is eating at you? What are you involved in and with whom?

Mother

Your mother represents many different things to you. She is your teacher and has set the example of the role of the female in relationship to men, children, relatives, sisters, brothers, even her own parents.

You must first understand what your mother represents to you. You may be the exact opposite of your mother. However, your relationship to your mother gives you an indication of the method you seek for acceptance and approval from people.

If you are a female and are like your mother, you seek approval based on a "goody-two-shoes" approach. This would indicate that your mode of acceptance and approval is based on straight acceptance.

On the other hand, if you are the exact opposite of your mother you may discover that your methodology for gaining acceptance and approval is through the avenue of rejection.

Although that seems counterproductive and counterintuitive, rejection is a form of approval. The difference between these two types is based on the nature of the relationship you have with your mother or the nature of the circumstances surrounding your conception and birth. If there was an unwanted pregnancy or difficulty with carrying and then delivery, rejection may be part of the issue.

If you are a male you will be like your mother's ideas of what a man should be. Look at your father. Are you like him or the opposite? Again, the two different forms of approval will determine your actions, attitudes and beliefs in the material plane.

Motherboard

When the motherboard on your computer goes out it renders your ability to communicate useless. Question what is going on that would interfere with your ability to communicate and facilitate things unfolding the way that you think they should or the way that you would like them to be.

Your computer could be tied into your vehicle of expression. You could use it for business purposes or part of your entertainment, your relaxation, or your escape. It could be used for all of the aforementioned.

You need to question what role the computer plays in your life and know that the motherboard is what everything else is built upon.

It is interesting that it is very much like "mother," which is also worth reading to help you gain some insights.

Mountain

Mountains can have different symbolic meanings. On one level, it signifies obstacles to overcome; the other is that it becomes a defensive position. Also, if you have ever climbed a mountain, it could be a symbol of accomplishment and overcoming a major obstacle.

Look around and see what obstacles you are facing that you must either climb over, find a way around, or barrel through. Perseverance is essential in all matters in life, especially when you are presented with an obstacle.

From a defensive point of view, if you build on the top of the mountain, you have a 360-degree view and can see anything coming at you from a distance. What an awareness to be able to see all the subtle energies at work. Symbols in your dreams help you do exactly that.

Mouth

The mouth gives the ability to express Self in all situations. It represents the ability to break down thoughts (chewing) for better utilization. Material sustenance begins here. Your mouth is part of your expression as well as your image.

Movie

Movies are a form of entertainment and/or escape. The type of movies you are attracted to is another symbol in itself. If it is a particular movie that is in question, you should go a step further and into the personal emotional associations that are attached to this film and its genre.

Muscles

Your muscles move everything in your body. When you think a thought it is converted into electrical energy. The action is then carried out instantly, unconsciously.

How you think is how you act. Muscles are symbolic of personal power and one's ability to handle situations.

Difficulties here would need to be examined from the point of view as to what part of the body is being affected.

N

Naked

Being naked implies being exposed and defenseless. In children, it represents innocence because they have not formed any real attitudes or opinions from a sexual perspective as adults do.

Look around and see what is going on that makes you feel exposed, defenseless, unprotected or conceivably threatened.

What does being naked mean to you? Is it dirty, shameful or perverse?

Neck

Balance between the spiritual (the head) and material (the torso) aspects of Self. The voice box located here.

Issues here indicate imbalance. In what ways are you approaching something that is imbalanced; not well thought out on all levels?

Is there someone or something that is giving you a pain in the neck? What is that about? What is going on?

Nervous system

Your skin and nervous system work together gathering and transmitting data of what is being experienced externally. The data that is gathered is simultaneously transmitted to the brain where it is processed according to the most prevalent concept at work at the moment.

Thoughts direct movement. All incoming data are compared to conceptual precepts, which are the ideas that you maintain about your Self and your reality. The data is converted from mental thought energies into action energies.

The nervous system is symbolic of communication on an internal level. Problems in this arena are because people may believe that they cannot "handle" a situation, or "stand up" to life. They may also believe that they do not have the strength to deal with certain levels of stress.

News

You would not think that this would require a symbolic interpretation. However, it depends on the type of news and who is delivering it.

In your dreams, the person or thing delivering the news is as important as the message being delivered. Is it coming through the radio, television, newspapers or magazines? In what way do you relate to the news? Do you have to write articles about the news? Do you write news? Are you a news commentator?

Like all symbols, thought has to be given as to how this particular thing relates to you.

Newt

See Lizard and Chameleon.

Nickel

Nickel represents two things. It is a mineral and it is a piece of currency, a coin of the realm. Nickels could represent material sustenance; very little, but sustenance all the same, especially if you have nothing, it is something.

There could be something with a nickel collection. This would be another personal situation.

Nickels also represent the number five. Five of what? Five of who? In what way does the number five relate to what you are going through?

Night

The night is a time of recuperation and preparation. From a recuperative point of view, when you go to sleep, that is when your body is doing its repair work, because certain systems become more active and dominant while other systems calm down and relax. The mind, on the other hand, is constantly awake and aware.

The night is where dreams come in, because your mind is assessing everything that took place during the previous day and is beginning to implement particular patterns of behavior because a subconscious concept has been stimulated by something during the day's events. That concept is now active and the pattern of behavior is beginning to manifest.

Your mind, in seeing that, will give you a dream that will tell you exactly what is on the way, where you are in the pattern, and what you need to do to adjust yourself to change the outcome.

Nightmares

This is a situation where guidance has been so suppressed that the dream mechanism has not been utilized and has become rusty. A nightmare is the vehicle used in order to grab your attention. This is something that requires immediate thought, analysis, questioning, seeking, understanding the symbology and becoming aware of what is going on in order to avoid problems and difficulties.

Look around and question, "What is going on? Why am I having these experiences?"

Noose

When you see a noose you think of a hanging. Based on that, you can make the association with death. First and foremost, death is the end of a cycle and symbolic of rejection. Keep in mind that every end is but a new beginning.

The question comes up, when has a noose been something in your life that you would create a PEA? What was that something and how does that relate to what you are going through and where you are in your life at this moment in time?

Nose

Used for the intake of fresh, clean air (symbolic of Spirit) and the exhaling of toxins. It is a protective aspect of the body being able to distinguish healthful or detrimental scents (truths). Faith in Self is also affected when one has respiratory issues.

The nose is also tied into image. In what way are you concerned about the appearance of your nose? Is it the appropriate size for your face? Are you comfortable with the look of it?

Numbers

The symbolic significance of numbers is based on the Universal Teachings. Numbers play a major role in life. They are even more important when you begin to look at them from the symbolic perspective. Numbers show up in dreams, events and even in daily occurrences.

When you have a dream you are getting guidance. This guidance, in the form of symbols, is based on your emotional associations and is designed to help you navigate the energies of the upcoming day. For instance, if you see three pens on a desk in your dream, it could indicate that there is a need to understand that there is something going on with your ability to communicate. Pens, from a symbolic perspective, could represent communication, especially for one who writes for a living.

Of course, that is the universal perspective. Your PEA may be different. That is one reason that it is in your best interest to create your own symbolic dictionary.

The same symbol may not mean the same thing to everyone. The pens could be an expression of art, drawing. The desk in our example may represent authority for one person and expression for someone else.

If you see more than one of anything in your dream, or your conscious reality, you need to look at it from the symbolic point of view. It will help to define exactly where you are in your cycle. It may even help you to see and understand what particular pattern is at work.

Before you go forward, realize that I chose only to put down the positive interpretations. It would be in your best interest to think also of the exact opposite in your interpretations at the same time. If you see everything through a positive interpretation without considering the possibility that the exact opposite is true, then you are living and looking at life through "rose-colored glasses." When you do that, you will be unprepared for the negative aspects should they be in the process of unfolding. Forewarned is forearmed.

Here are the numbers to help you begin to think in these terms.

1 = Unity.
Unity within the Self between the male and the female aspects and the material and spiritual aspects of Self

2 = Balance and Harmony.
1+1=2. When you have unity between the male and female, as well as the material and spiritual, you have true balance and harmony.

3 = Understanding.
2+1=3. When you are in unity with Self and are in balance and harmony, you understand whatever you are confronting.

4 = Advancement.
3 + 1 =4. When you are in unity with Self and understand, you advance in life on the path of mastery.

2 + 2 =4. When you are in balance and harmony within your material and spiritual Self and your male and female Self, you advance in life on the path to mastery.

5 = Material Plane.
It is through the five senses that you are connected to the material plane.
4 + 1 =5. When you are in unity and are advancing, you are in control of your emotions and material existence.

3 + 2 =5. When you are in balance and harmony and incorporating understanding in your endeavors, you are in control of your emotions and material existence.

6 = Man.

Man was created on the sixth day. Man is given dominion over the material plane. (Genesis 1:26)

5 + 1 =6. When you approach the material plane in unity, you are being Man, both male and female.

4 + 2 =6. When you are advancing in your life from the position of balance and harmony, you are Man.

3 + 3 =6. When your understandings, both male and female as well as material and spiritual, guide you, you are Man.

7 = Cycle.

The heavens (Spirit) and Earth (material) were created in seven days. Everything in the universe flows in cycles. Your personal history repeats itself just as the cliché states, "History repeats itself." You can be in control of the outcome of each cycle in your life depending on how you enter into it. Symbols are the guideposts that can keep you on the path.

6 + 1 =7. Man in total unity starts every cycle in life from a position of strength.

5 + 2 =7. In the material plane, when you are in balance and harmony you start each cycle from a position of Strength.

4 + 3 =7. When you are in understanding and advancing, you start each cycle in life from a position of Strength.

8 = Mastery of the Material Plane

7 + 1 = 8. Entering a cycle in total unity leads to total mastery of the material plane.

6 + 2 = 8. Man as master of self and being in balance and harmony will master the material plane.

5 + 3 = 8. Totally understanding the material plane and your relationship within it leads to mastery.

4 + 4 = 8 Advancement upon advancement leads to total material mastery.

9 = Cleansing.

There are nine openings in the body for bringing in fresh clean food, such as air, water, foodstuff and thoughts. If you do not eliminate the refuse, that which is no longer useful; you will become toxic and die. What thoughts are being retained at a subconscious level that may be toxic? (Openings: nose, ears, eyes, mouth, anus, and urethra.)

8 + 1 = 9. Mastery of life and true unity require a constant cleansing process to ensure continued growth and development.

7 + 2 = 9. Starting a new cycle in strength and balance and harmony requires a constant cleansing process to ensure continued growth and development.

6 + 3 = 9. Man can only achieve true understanding through the internal cleansing process. Understanding the motivating factors at work on a subconscious level gives Man an opportunity to gain control over his/her emotional life and thus truly master life.

5 + 4 = 9. True advancement in the material plane requires a constant cleansing process to ensure continued growth and development.

10 = Handling.

You have ten fingers to grip, hold, and manipulate material life; ten fingers to handle any situation you are in. You are never placed in a situation that you cannot master. You have ten toes, five on each foot; these are for balancing you on your path. Without toes to balance you, standing erect and having a strong position in matters of life would be difficult.

$9 + 1 = 10$. When you cleanse the negative beliefs and expectations you maintain about yourself and become in unity with your Self, you can handle anything.

$8 + 2 = 10$. With degrees of mastery and being in balance and harmony, you can handle anything.

$7 + 3 = 10$. Going into any cycle with understanding will allow you to handle anything that might arise.

$6 + 4 = 10$. Man is meant to advance in each life cycle. You have the tools to handle anything that would block your growth and development.

$5 + 5 = 10$. By keeping the material plane in its proper perspective, and maintaining balance, one can handle all situations masterfully.

O

Oboe

An oboe is a musical instrument. Like all musical instruments it has the commonality of seeking to participate in balance and harmony as part of a team.

Beyond that, it would take greater understanding of an oboe to go further into its symbology. I would assume that if it is in your dream it has a personal association for you.

Octagon

An octagon is an eight-sided object. The number 8 is the number of the material plane; it makes me think that there is an opportunity at hand.

You may be in the center of an octagon or you may be on the outside walking around it and looking for a way in. In either case, it may be obscured from you because you cannot see all eight sides at once unless you get above it or beneath it.

From that perspective, maybe an overview is necessary of everything that is going on. What opportunities surround you? What opportunities are you in the middle of and you do not see? Look harder. Alter your perception. Approach it from a different point of view.

Octopus

An octopus is an ocean creature with tentacles that capture its prey for consumption. The question arises, how do you extend tentacles out to people to entrap or ensnare them?

They could also be a communication system among the octopus in order to identify what is what.

Are these creatures part of your expression? Do you earn a living in some way that relates to them?

Orange

Orange is both a color and a fruit. As a fruit, it is know to be high in vitamin C. So we could say that it is symbolic of nourishment, sunshine, which could take you to a number of different places depending on your relationship with sunshine. Look for a PEA here. See Colors for another perspective on the color orange.

Orbit

To orbit something is to circle it. Are you going around in circles? What or who are you orbiting? Where is it taking you? Or are you orbiting in an upward spiral? If you are not, work with your dreams and you will discover how to alter the flow and outcome of your patterns of behavior.

Currently, for most people, their cycles are running horizontally, which is why their personal history keeps repeating itself. If you want to change your history, the regular outcome of your patterns of behavior, then reading symbols and changing attitudes based on insights gained will allow for the changing of the outcome of your pattern.

A new outcome will start you on the spiral path. As long as you continue to pay attention, read symbols and apply the understandings, there will be growth and mastery.

Orchestra

An orchestra is a vehicle of expression, as well as a symbol expressive of harmony and balance. If you enjoy listening to an orchestra, it is a symbol of entertainment. If you are part of the orchestra, it is a symbol of expression.

It may be that it was a way to spend time with one of your parents, which would be a thing of joy and pleasure. Or it was something you were forced to do, in which case it is a symbol of imposition.

Do you play an instrument? Did you try out for the orchestra and were accepted, or perhaps rejected?

Ostrich

Is your head in the sand? Is there something you do not want to see? Ostriches will do two things, as people do. They will either run from danger, which may be an intelligent thing to do. Or they will act out of fear, in which case they may bury their head in the sand, hoping it will pass them by. If they do not see it, they do not have to react to it. With that type of response, there may be devastation.

In what way does an ostrich relate to what you are going through? In what way would an ostrich be part of your expression? Was it a pet? Is it sustenance? Is it something you earn a living from?

Ostriches are flightless birds. Do you have certain thoughts that cannot take flight? Maybe you are burying your head in the sand out of doubt and uncertainty and cannot see how to get it off the ground or find another avenue to express your desire.

Outside

The outside could be symbolic of freedom or exposure. Depending what you are outside of, there may be no one who is watching or has anything to say about what you are doing. You are completely free to go and be and do whatever you want.

Being outside also means that you are exposed to the natural elements. The question is what are the elements at work in your life? Go back and look at the definition of elements to understand what energies may be at work in your life.

Outer Self

Outer Self, is the result of your belief system. We call the Ego the Outer Self because it comprises all the images you believe you should be, or expect yourself to be. That belief and expectation is predominately based on man-made teachings. The outer mantel is built upon a façade, built upon the Ego, a level of consciousness of the Self that you show the world all day long. It is your reflection of your constant awareness of everything that is going on in your life

Outerwear

See Coat.

Ovaries

These glands deal with the maturing process of the body. They stimulate, prepare and maintain the body for reproductive expression.

The symbology involved here includes self-image and expression. The inability to have children is often tied to concepts surrounding immaturity, lack of authority, fear of responsibility, lack of self-expression and self-worth to mention a few of the energies that could be at work preventing fertilization.

Oversized

When something is oversized it is too big for its intended purpose. If you find yourself in oversized clothing, or an oversized home or vehicle, you have to question what it is that you are trying to create that is oversized for the task at hand. Is it overkill where it is too much? If so, the Universal Teaching of, "Excess leads to rejection," will become a dominant force in the transaction.

Do you feel things are oversized? Do you have trouble bringing things down to size? These are additional considerations that need to be brought into the mix.

Oxen

Oxen are one of the "beasts of burden" that do all the work. They pull the plow and the wagons; they turned the wheel to crush the grain. What part of you is the ox, a beast of burden? What are you burdened by?

Try to see it from a different point of view. It may reveal an insight that will lead to an understanding and that will change everything.

Oxygen

Oxygen is symbolic of life and, therefore, symbolic of spirit. You need oxygen to live and you need spirit to live. How is the oxygen being presented? Is it in a tank? Are you under an oxygen tent in an intensive care unit? Are you starving for oxygen? Are you in a high atmosphere where the oxygen is thin?

All of these considerations must be woven into the entire communication that is being presented to you by your mind.

P

Pair

What is the pair you are looking at or are involved with? Is it a pair of something? Are you part of a pair? Is the pair composed of twins? In what way does this pair relate to you?

Consider also that a pair indicates two, which could be a duality in the sense of opposites, as well as duality in that two separate opportunities are being presented. Maybe you have to choose between one and another. Maybe you are caught up in a pair that should not be.

See how it relates to what you are going through. As always, this is the key ingredient. What am I going through and how does this relate to me?

Pancreas

This gland produces enzymes for digestion of food. It also produces insulin. The pancreas is symbolic of your ability to take certain thoughts and ideas and make them work. They can provide you with the fuel (courage and strength) to carry on.

Panties

Panties are protective garments. Whose panties are they? What is the style? Are they baggy cotton balloons or are they thongs? Are you wearing them in the dream or is someone else wearing them? Are they your panties? Are you concerned about the whole concept of panties and someone getting into your panties?

There are all kinds of issues here because of the intimacy of where panties are worn, so it raises questions of expression on that level with those types of considerations.

Pants

Pants are a protective covering. Women might wear them in the winter for warmth and protection from the elements. It is standard dress for men, especially for business.

What kind of pants are they? Are they dress or casual slacks or jeans? Are they torn, dirty, clean, pressed? Every element needs to be dissected and questioned.

Paper

Paper may be used as part of your expression. It could be tied into homework or business. You may sell paper or you may use it to write, draw or paint.

In what way is the paper appearing in your dream, and in what way do you utilize paper in your daily life? Does that have any relevance to the rest of the dream? Is there something special about paper to you?

Again, this is a personal emotional association that will bring greater clarity to something so common and simple.

Parathyroid

This gland maintains normal blood levels, and regulates the metabolism of calcium and phosphorus. The parathyroid ensures that there is a steady and stable supply of it.

Blood is symbolic of spiritual life. Calcium is symbolic of strength. Phosphorus is symbolic of inspiration/courage. By affecting the metabolism of these two minerals, the parathyroid provides the body (Self) with the courage to continue. Regardless of what level a person is on, or what situation they are in. Without courage and inspiration, the strength is not there to help handle situations and the subsequent growth.

Pear

As a fruit, you can go to the concept of sustenance. However, there may be a personal emotional association. You might be allergic to pears. You may grow them. You may like pear jams or jellies.

Try to understand the relationship of pears to whatever it is. Are you looking at a fruit bowl and it only has pears?

Pen

A pen can be a form of expression. But, if you do not have a job where you utilize a pen in your work, it is not an issue. However, if you have a pen and you write letters or you write poetry, or you pay bills every day, then it becomes a tool of expression. It depends on how you use a pen or pencil. If and when you lose it, it becomes an issue. Then the questions become, "How did I misplace my expression? What's going on in my life that I am unclear about my expression? Why can't I find my expression?" See also Vehicles of Expression.

Pencil

A pencil, like a pen, is related to the vehicle of expression. How do you utilize a pencil in your expressions?

Consider that one difference between a pen and a pencil is that you can erase anything you write with a pencil. With a pen, you cannot. (Assuming it is not erasable ink.) Pencils, therefore, may be of a temporary nature in expression and communication.

Perhaps, on some level, it could represent an immature form of expression because children write more with pencils than adults. Adults use pens because of the certainty of their minds, whereas children are still learning and may not be so clear about things. See also Vehicles of Expression.

Penny

Pennies represent sustenance and the ability to purchase something, if you have enough. They are the lowest common element in our system of money. Where is the penny appearing in your dream? How is it appearing? How many pennies are there? Remember, whenever anything appears you have to look at the number of units being presented to you, and then look at the symbology of the number of units.

Perky

When you think of someone being perky, you think of youthful exuberance. You could say this represents immaturity and excitement. What is going on that is causing the perkiness and could be exciting? In what ways are you acting immature? Are you acting perky and is it appropriate for what is going on?

Pest

Pests can be insects, such as mosquitoes. They are annoying, irritating, distracting and could be carriers of disease.

They could also be people who fit all those categories. Who or what is the pest? In what way is it pestering you? How does that relate to what you are currently going through?

Phone

See Telephone. See also Vehicles of Expression.

Pin

See Tack.

Place

Sanctuary, reprieve, hideaway, destination, entertainment, escape; it depends on the place. Be it a landmark, amusement park or state park, it all comes down to what that particular place means to you. When was it a part of your life? What associations are you making with it and how does that relate to what you are going through?

Plane

Unless you are the pilot, when you are on a plane you are at the pilot's mercy. You are inactive, but it is still a vehicle taking you from one place to another.

If you fly regularly on business, it would be one connotation. If you are afraid to get on a plane, that is another. If your only experiences were tragic, that is another one. If you only fly for vacations, that is yet another.

You can begin to see the different applications of looking at something, because the same point of view holds true in so many different aspects of the things you look at.

Plasma

Plasma is a liquid that contains many different elements depending on the type of plasma it is. In regards to your own blood stream, plasma contains all the ions, gases and nutrients the cells require for health. The blood cells carry oxygen. They are the life providers of the body because without oxygen your life would cease.

Look at the plasma in plants. Chlorophyll is the same as blood from a molecular point of view. The major difference between human blood and chlorophyll is that blood has an iron atom and chlorophyll has a magnesium one. Iron carries oxygen and magnesium facilitates electrical conductivity.

Playing

Playing is another youthful attribute and a sign of immaturity based on man's concept of what is mature, as in you are not supposed to have a good time and not supposed to be playing after a certain age.

However, playing is a form of expression, as well. You also have a different kind of play where you learn lines and perform. From that perspective, if you find yourself as a character in a play, you should ask what kind of character you are playing and how it relates to you. You can begin to see all the questions that would arise from that sort of episode.

Playpen

Playpens are built for restriction, confinement, safety, and security. A playpen could be part of role-playing in some way, in which case the depth of understanding the words of confinement go a little bit further.

Pollen

You could be allergic to pollen. As seeds of germination, what are you in the thinking stages of that is going to require some outside help in order to germinate and bear fruit to your thoughts and ideas?

As an allergen, pollen could be considered an irritant. Depending upon what type of pollen you are allergic to, this would give some greater insights as to what may be going on. It is interesting that pollen is carried from plant to plant by bees, and carried back to the hive to produce food. Pollen is a protein.

It would pay to understand the symbology of protein, which is, fundamentally, building blocks. What is going on that may require you to consume pollen as a way of building your internal strength, perseverance, and qualities that are essential in bringing to fruition anything you seek to germinate?

Porpoise

A porpoise is a mammal that lives in the ocean, related to the dolphin and whale. On one level, a porpoise could be an expression within the material plane that has learned to adapt in both the material-spiritual world and the material-physical world exemplified by the ocean.

Do you have a personal association with this creature? Do you care for them? Is it part of your expression through some form of art?

Prostate

In males, the prostate gland helps regulate urine flow. It also aids in the reproductive system. Because it is tied into these systems, it is affected by subconscious concepts that deal with expression of manhood and self-image.

Puke

Whatever the thought was, it was repulsive and something you could not tolerate or stomach, or you were unwilling to digest it and incorporate it into your life.

The normal tendency for most people is to immediately say that it is physical, i.e. something bad that they ate. Consider the fact that your mind led you to that food or drink item. It is in touch with everything. Everything is energy.

Your mind sensed that there was a particular energy out there that it could use to communicate with you. Therefore, it had you choose bad food in order to drive the point home because you were still entertaining some aspect of what was being presented, yet you knew subconsciously that it was diametrically opposed to you. Because you missed all the other symbols that were alerting you about the indigestion aspect of these thoughts, you continued forward. Therefore, your mind had to go to the next level.

Purple

Purple is the color of royalty. This stems from the fact that in ancient times approximately 12,000 shellfish were needed to make 1.5 grams of purple dye, making it extremely rare and expensive. Therefore, items utilizing purple dye were accessible only to the wealthy.

Purple Haze

A purple haze indicates a distorted view of something. In a

haze, clarity is hindered. You may be able to make out shapes and forms, but you cannot be clear about what or who they are and what they represent until they come closer.

On some levels, this means that if you are looking through a haze then you are very vulnerable because you have only a short time in which to protect your Self from what could be a devastating attack or loss.

Purpose

Purpose can mean a direction or calling. To have purpose is to have a goal. If something is purposeful, it may be tied into having a goal or something to do. Maybe your mind is telling you that you need to find purpose.

Purse/Wallet

More often than not you carry your money, credit cards and identification in your purse. See Handbag.

Putrid

This is a smell with which it is easy to make an emotional association because it leaves a biting memory. If you are having this experience in a meditative state, smell it in a dream or if it comes to you while you are seeking a vision, then the question is: When was the last time you smelled this and the time before that?

Each of those will denote the fact that you are in a similar cycle as before, so the same pattern of behavior is operating and you need to understand what it is because you obviously missed other symbols leading up to this.

Q

Quarter

A quarter is a coin of the realm. From that perspective, you could say that a quarter could provide sustenance. How many quarters are there? What do quarters represent to you?

On the other hand, it could be one-fourth of something. What does that type of quarter represent to you? In what way does it provide you with sustenance? Or, do you feel you are being gypped out of something? There are many different considerations for the quarter.

R

Rabbits

The most common association with rabbits is their renowned ability to procreate. With that in mind, the symbolic interpretation would start with reproduction. Another word might be propagation, which would have a different meaning.

Rabbits propagate very readily and, apparently, very easily. If so, you could ask, "What thoughts have I been propagating?" What new actions, new directions are being stimulated? What were you involved in yesterday that rabbits would be saying to you that, conceivably, you must propagate more thoughts because this is going to require more than one to move through this? It is going to require a brood or family of thoughts.

Rabbits can also be good luck. People used to carry a rabbit's foot for good luck. Rabbits also have the ability to blend in with the environment. Not like a chameleon that changes colors, but it has a good basic camouflage and it is fast. It does not walk, it hops, which is a different mode of transportation.

Whatever it is you were going through, or whoever it is that this symbol applies to, may very well need to think in terms of propagating thoughts; moving on them, hopping through it, and not meander about trying to get to where you are going. Pick your direction and hop to it. Look at it from that perspective.

Rabbits are also excellent listeners. Their ears are great for listening for the sounds of life and danger because they are also a prey. They are food for others. Maybe there is a need to pay attention and listen clearly to what is going on and try to have your senses about you. You would have to tie that into whatever you are going through.

Above and beyond all of that, you would have to remember back in your childhood if you ever had a pet rabbit, or if you grew up in an environment where there were rabbits and you perhaps ate them. There may be some deep emotional association with that.

Brer Rabbit

Brer Rabbit is a storybook character that may represent comfort. That is another aspect to the beauty of symbology. The more you can understand your emotional relationship to it, the clearer the communication will be. For instance, if Brer Rabbit was a favorite story that your grandparents read to you and it gave you a sense of security and belonging, then seeing those rabbits could mean that your need to feel that way is present.

Raft

Another vehicle of expression; as a passenger you are at the mercy of the driver. You are subject to the concepts of whoever is in the driver's seat.

A raft is a vehicle for traversing over water. Water being symbolic of the material plane, your material considerations are foremost of importance in this dream symbol. Where is it that you are trying to get to materially? In the same respect, you are seeking to do so without being deeply involved in this particular material pursuit. See also Vehicles of Expression.

Rails

There are different ways to look at rails because there are different applications. On one level, you have the rails for a trolley, a subway, or a train. Which rails indicate in that situation is a movement you are locked into? There is no turning right or left and no veering. There is only traveling in the direction of the rails.

Where are the rails taking you? Where are you coming from? What is restricting your freedom one way or another in terms of making a turn, an adjustment?

In one sense, rails lock you in. Another definition of rails could mean a railing around a pool area, which can lock you in or out. There are handrails on stairs to help you ascend or descend. In what way are rails showing up in your dream? Do you need support in ascending? Do you need the security in descending? Do you need to create a rail around yourself? How do you create rails around yourself that are locking you in and/or locking people out?

Keep your mind open as to the definition of rails and see how it applies to the other symbols within the dream sequence.

Rain

Rain is another word with multiple applications. Rain feeds the earth, it provides water, it nourishes plants, and it may be something that makes you feel good because it may bring back childhood memories. Maybe you used to love watching the rain or thunder and lightning storms. Maybe the rain was an imposition because when it rained you were locked in and forbidden to go out, so it hindered your enjoyment.

Rain is going to be one of those things you are going to have a personal emotional association with depending upon the way you relate to it and what was occurring in the dream.

Red

The color red represents anger and danger. This is one of the reasons that stop signs are painted red, a sign of danger.

What is red in your dream? Is it a sign of danger? Is it a sign of emotions?

When emotions are out of control, you absolutely have danger. See what object or person is red and how it applies to what is going on. Do you need to come to a stop on a particular action you are taking?

These are things worthy of questioning. You see so many people with red sports cars. They are conveying a certain image. So, red can also be tied into an attitude of, "Look at me. Notice me. Acknowledge me."

Refrigerator

This appliance is generally found in the kitchen. The refrigerator is one appliance where you store your sustenance. When it breaks down there is a problem. Conceivably, that which you have stored may deteriorate, rot, that which you have confidence in, that which you think is going to support you may be in danger of not supporting you. How does that apply to what is taking place?

Reptile

Go back to the story that takes place in the Garden of Eden, where you see how a reptile tricked Eve into eating the apple. In truth, reptiles are phallic symbols, and it is the expression of manhood that will always lead one astray.

What is the reptile in this particular vision, dream or experience? What kind of a reptile? Is it a snake? Is it a lizard? What is it, what is it doing, and how does it relate to you and how do you relate to it? Is there fear associated with snakes? Have you had a snake for a pet?

These are some of the considerations that need to be brought into play when you are examining a dream. It is like a painter using different hues to create the picture they want to express.

Retarded growth

Retarded growth can be related to personality, emotions, or physical stature. These do not necessarily have to connect to human beings. Retardation simply means to hold back, to slow down.

If you are surrounded by retarded things in your dream, then ask what these things represent to you. In what way do you feel they are holding you back from moving forward? Do you feel retarded? In what arena do you feel less than everyone else? What is going on with all that you are seeing in relation to the concept of retardation?

Ring

Rings have many different definitions. There is the ring of a bell. What does a ringing bell mean to you? When was it a part of your life? What does the particular ringing you heard mean to you? Do you have any emotional association with it?

What about the rings on your fingers? Your fourth finger is symbolic of social ties and identities. It is where you wear your school ring or your wedding ring, which are social statements. In today's fashion there are people with rings on every finger on their hand. What does that say? Is that another way of saying, "Look at me? Look at my gold, my diamonds, and my jewelry. Look how successful I am. Look how powerful I am."

Do you have a ring through your nose or your ears? What rings do you have on your hands?

What about the ring around a bathtub or sink? This usually implies dirt, poverty or slovenly behavior.

These are all things to be taken into consideration when one is interpreting a dream. There is no single definition. As you have seen by looking at the different things in this book, words have so many different meanings and such depth that if you do not explore deep enough, you are liable to miss the value of the communication and the importance of what is being said to you.

Right Side

Spiritual intent, the right side symbolizes spiritual thoughts and actions, your faith in Self as it relates to a situation. It represents the future, as well. The right side is considered the female aspect of the Self, the intuitive.

Ritz

Think of elegance. The Ritz Carlton hotels are a great example.

"They are Ritzy," or "It's a ritzy restaurant." One makes the associations with upscale living or upscale presentation. How does that fit into what you are going through? Is it something you want to portray, if so, why? Do you feel that being ritzy or staying at The Ritz, or living ritzy makes you a better person?

It just says that you have money, and money does not mean that you are a better person. Being a better person is exemplified by the love, kindness, care and consideration you put out in your daily life. It is how you deal with people.

River

Rivers are moving bodies of water. They have different levels of depth, as well as speeds of flow. Rivers symbolically represent an element of material life.

Go back to a point in time when, as a child, you may have lived somewhere where a river was your place of solitude, it was your place of comfort, a place to go to, to run to, to interact with, that gave you a sense of peace or a sense of security.

However, I would probably look at it from the perspective that there is something going on in your life in which the flow of thoughts and concerns is in the material. Maybe some issues are flowing towards you that will require your energy to get under control.

Are you immersed in the river? Are you floating or boating on the river? Are you swimming? All of these actions will provide even greater insights and understandings as to the energies at work.

Road

Roads can be long or short, wide or narrow, as well as winding. They can lead you downhill or uphill. You have to understand the nature of the road.

Fundamentally, a road is a path that takes you from one place to another. How does that tie into your dream? Where are you coming from? Do you have a short way to go to get to where you want to go, or is it going to be a long haul? Are there going to be a lot of twists and turns?

The dream is feeding you information based on what occurred yesterday or even the day before, and it is letting you know how to traverse the particular road you are on.

Roads can also represent a transition, going from one place to another. Destinations do not necessarily mean physical places. They could be states of consciousness. Examine this as thoroughly as possible to get the deepest understanding.

Rocks or Stones

First examine little rocks and stones. Those are defenses and they are the defenses that you generally attack with, because you throw stones at people. In fact, the old custom was to stone people to death for their transgressions.

Larger boulders and stones could be greater defenses, because you can take them and build walls around your reality. Bigger stones and boulders, which you could call hills or mountains, would be obstacles in your life.

Have you been knocked off your boulder that you have been sitting on and find yourself on the ground; then it is possible that you are going to be knocked off your lofty position and be knocked off a defensive position simultaneously.

Boulders were used to build fortresses on top of mountains because they were inaccessible. "You cannot attack me if I am up here, so it is my defense structure." Getting knocked off of it is obvious that there is a force at work that is undermining your footing in terms of your defensive posture.

Another part of that could be that you are losing the ability to maintain an objective perspective on things, because a boulder is also something that you climb on in order to see. However, if you are sitting there, then it raises other questions. Are you observing or are you holding court? Holding court in a sense that I am up here, you are all down there, I am in control, this is my position, and then someone comes along and knocks you off your position.

Look at that and relate it to what you are going through to see what forces were at work to dethrone you, unseat you, or push you off your position, and then go from that perspective.

Ropes

Ropes are used to tie things, to bundle, tie up loose ends, capture something, or control something. How are the ropes being used in this particular vision or dream? Are you immersed in something? Are you wrapped up by ropes? Or, are you holding on to the end of a rope? If so, what is on the other end of the rope? Is it taking you someplace, or are you pulling the rope in to bring something to you? Have you used the rope as a lasso to capture something? Are you trying to tie someone or something up? What else is in the dream that will give you insight on how to best utilize that rope to that advantage?

Rulers

Depending upon the dream and the ruler you are seeing; is it 12 inches? A yardstick? A triangular ruler? Is it a folding carpenter's ruler? Is it a roll-up tape measure?

What are you trying to measure? By what measurement are you looking at things? In what way are you measuring things? What needs to be measured?

Rulers can also be kings or queens. In that regard, they represent authority. These are positions of authority that can rule you. Who is the king or queen in your life? Do they rule you? How do you feel about their stewardship?

Rules

Rules are something you have to live by. There are rules and regulations of proper etiquette, for instance. Rules are statements of how one should act and be in a societal and civilized way.

What are you going through and what are the rules you are being asked to follow? What are the rules you are breaking and why? "Why?" is the best question you can ask yourself, no matter what is going on.

Every time you ask that question, it is going to take you someplace else and to another question. Every question does have an answer. Hopefully, the questioning you are doing is taking you into your Self. Why am I going through this? Why am I like this? Why did I say that? Why did I do this? Why didn't I do that?

You can see the power of "Why?" It is something you should embrace because it will be a key that will unlock many mysteries of the Self.

Rural/Country Roads

Along with country roads, rural also denotes uncivilized. It is not a city or community. It is out in the sticks in the rural environment. Not necessarily primitive, but maybe more self-sufficient; living off of the grid.

What does rural mean to you and how is it applicable to what is currently going on in your life? Did you grow up in a rural environment? Do you want to live in a rural environment? Do you want to get away from the city?

Does rural imply escape to you and do you want to escape? Everything implies something and symbology helps you seek out what you are going through to understand so you can have greater insights into the Self, which will lead you on the path to mastery.

❧

S

Saw

There are all kinds of saws: Hand saws, hacksaws, table saws. What kind of saw was in your dream? A saw cuts things to size. It can be used to cut planks out of a tree trunk for construction. What kind of a saw is in your hand? Is it a saw to cut through cement? Is it a hacksaw to cut through metal or iron?

In what way are saws a part of your life? Are saws parts of your personal expression? Are you a carpenter, a builder or a contractor where saws are an important piece of equipment for you? How do you have an emotional association with a saw?

Seek to understand this in relationship to the other symbols within the dream or vision to see what it is you are trying to cut down to size. What is going on? Is there something you need to build up so that you need to saw wood, steel, etc. in order to create whatever it is you want to create?

Scorpions

Scorpions are creatures with the capacity to sting, most of which live in dark, rotted wood places. How does that relate to you? Did you ever have a scorpion as a pet? Were you ever stung by a scorpion? Is the scorpion part of your astrological sign? Do you feel you have been stung by someone who is a threat to you?

Seeds

Seeds grow things. They are thoughts and attitudes. They are

202 Dream Symbology Dictionary

condensed life. Seeds are sustenance. You can eat sunflower seeds and pumpkin seeds. You can sprout many different types of seeds for sustenance. Seeds can be planted to bring forth life and to bring forth protection.

What seeds were in your dream and in what way do you relate to seeds? Is gardening a pastime of yours? Is it some of your expression? How are the seeds related to what you are going through?

Serpent

A serpent is a reptile that lives in the ocean. This goes back to reptiles and the expression of manhood. You could also look at aggression, adversity and deceitfulness.

Remember that it was a reptile that "tricked" Eve into eating the apple from the Tree of Knowledge of Good and Evil. Of course, that story is a symbolic teaching of how man entered into the material plane. It was through the expression of manhood that mankind stayed here because he became enamored with the material plane and that was our fall from grace. Try to get a handle on the serpent outside of the suggestions here.

Shoes

Shoes have many symbolic interpretations because there are so many different types of shoes. For instance, the many styles of high heeled shoes for women convey different images. The particular symbology would depend on the type of heel that was being worn, as well as the specific style and color.

You may wear sandals as your favorite style of shoe, which would be another type of imagery. So shoes, all-in-all, are going to represent the image that you are projecting. Look at boots, rain or hiking shoes. These types of shoes are fully functional.

Physically and symbolically they may help you get a firmer stance or footing in a particular terrain. Shoes can also be a protective device.

Shoes become an important symbol in your dreams or in any given situation where your attention was drawn to them. For instance, you may have a dream where you are walking in the rain and trying to get somewhere or resolve an issue. In this instance, as you are interpreting the dream, the shoes have symbolic value in the sense that they convey a message. They give you some insight into what you will have to do.

The rain and the boots may indicate that you are going to be involved in some heavy material endeavor. I use the term "material" because of the symbology of water. Water is symbolic of the material plane or dimension.

An interpretation may take the form of, "Something is going on in my material direction that I am heading in that I may need some additional protection from the 'elements' of the situation or transactions."

In another dream you may put on hiking boots to help you go climbing. In this case, it is a matter of using a different type of footing in order to overcome an obstacle that is in your way. It will truly be something that you will need to ascend in order to get "above it."

Golf shoes offer another type of symbology. These give you better traction. So shoes, depending on the type you pay attention to, would be an indication of an additional consideration in the direction that you are moving.

Show or Play

Shows or plays are mainly fictional in nature. What are you involved in that may be fictional in the sense that it is a performance and you are on display? In what way does that fit into the rest of the symbology in the dream or vision and what is currently going on in your life?

A show or play could also be a form of escape. It could be a form of entertainment, as well as personal expression if you are involved in it.

Sieve/Drain

A sieve, like a colander, is something you use to drain things. If you wash your vegetables and fruits, you put them in a colander to drain.

A sieve, on the other hand, acts like a filter and pulls out particles that do not belong. What are you involved in that requires filtration? What do you have to sift through in order to get to the essence of what you are looking for?

Silver

Silver can denote wealth or debt, silver certificates, precious metal, or something of value. In what way do you have a personal association with silver? Does it provide security? Does it relate to a favorite piece of jewelry? You can see an emotional attachment from that perspective, as well.

Sister

When you see your sister in a dream, you are looking at another aspect of your Self. Remember, everyone in your dream is another aspect of your personality. What does your sister represent to you? Does she represent competition? Was she your older sister or younger sister? Did you idolize her or despise her? What are your emotional feelings toward your sister?

Skeletal System

The inner framework foundation of your body is the skeletal system. It is what you use to support yourself. The bones also produce blood, symbolic of the spiritual life of the Self and body in material form. Thoughts accepted and operated with, produce your blood.

Broken bones indicate a doubt in a particular area of your life. This is relevant to what you are going through or facing in your daily life at that given moment in time. In this case it is imperative to understand the symbology of the particular bone that is broken or bruised.

Skin

The skin is your physical contact point with the material world. It is through this sensory organ that you physically experience the world you live in. The skin also acts as a protective device against millions of microbes. Your skin also acts as a steam/toxic ventilator.

Your sensitivities to life are expressed here. The way you think influences how you are "touched" by certain situations, and how you react to them. Difficulties in this area usually stem from subconscious concepts of physical image, personal expression and the man-made role of the male and the female.

Skulls

Skulls have no eyes to see. Unlike a head, which has skin and hair, a skull is flesh-bare bone.

It could also be associated with death or the ending of a cycle or rejection. With no eyes to see, ears to hear or tongue to speak, a skull represents being deaf, dumb and blind.

When skulls appear in your dreams, ask yourself what is going on that makes you feel you have none of those attributes working for you. In fact, they may very well be working against you because you do not have the ability to discern subtleties without the ability of sight, sound and taste.

Snakes

Snakes are the "expression of manhood" from a universal perspective. This is so because a snake is a phallic symbol. Remember, it was the expression of manhood that got mankind in trouble in the Garden of Eden. It was the snake that convinced Eve to partake of the fruit from the Tree of Knowledge and that act of consumption symbolized our fall from grace.

There is more to the symbology of this story in the Bible. However, for our discussion on the symbology of snakes, suffice it to say that it is our expression of manhood that often leads us astray.

Look at how some folks express themselves. See how they laud their situation over others. They may use their money or power to influence or dominate a situation. This is an excellent example of "expression of manhood" in action.

Now, that does not necessarily mean that only men are prone to that because "manhood" constitutes male and female. God created man, male and female.[24]

Snakes can also represent fear. They also represent deviousness. When looking at a snake or any creature to understand its symbology, do not look at it from the way man normally views it. When you are looking at an animal, look at its habits, look at how it lives and sustains itself. How does it hunt? What does it do? Where does it live? These are the types of questions that will help you to understand the symbology.

A rattlesnake is a unique kind of a snake because it gives you a warning before it strikes. If a rattlesnake appears in your dream, you have to look at the other elements of the dream and everything else you are involved in. You may be involved in a situation where there is something devious afoot, something deceptive, something trying to lure you into a trap of sorts. Nor will the snake deliver what it promises to deliver. Yet, at the same time, you are being given a warning.

There are other warning signs telling you there is something going on. Obviously, there is something you are involved in based on the fact that you saw it in your dream. There is something you are involved in that requires a second look. Try to get a sure footing so that you are standing on solid ground with a clear view, and you will understand all of the elements involved.

There is another aspect to the symbology of the snake and it is tied into an expression that I am sure you are familiar with. It is about people who are considered to be a "snake in the grass." When this symbol occurs it requires examining the symbology of the grass, as well.

The grass has its own symbology because grass provides sustenance, provides herbs and grass is healing. Grass could also be camouflage, so you would have to look at the entire scene in order to truly understand what is being communicated to you from your subconscious mind. And everything is going to come back down to your personal emotional association with the symbols.

Symbols change as your understandings grow. Whenever a fear is manifesting in your life, it is manifesting because of a particular degree of a lack of confidence and knowledge. As you grow, your knowledge grows and the degree of fear diminishes because it is no longer at a particular vibratory rate.

For ease of example, let us say that the snake has a vibratory rate of 100; that rate is no longer applicable because now your fear is only vibrating at 98, so now you have to find a new symbol that vibrates at 98. Your symbols will change with your understanding, and with your experience.

With each endeavor, each new situation you are involved in, different degrees of fear or doubt are triggered. Because different levels are triggered you have different symbols for those levels. You could, theoretically, have up to 360 different symbols for doubt and fear. I say 360 because there are 360 degrees in a cycle or a circle. Each degree is an element of understanding. The more you understand, the more you conquer a fear. The more you confront a fear and a doubt, a force, you dissipate its energy. It no longer has power over you. That is the beauty of confronting your fears.

Move forward no matter what. As you do that you gain courage and confidence and all those other symbols disappear because they no longer have relevance in your consciousness, in your life, in your dictionary. So, yes, they do change.

Snow

Snow indicates a time change or new season, inconvenience or confinement, cold, unfriendly feelings or life threatening situations. Is it deep? Is it fresh? Is it dirty?

All of these considerations must be involved when one is deciphering a dream. Just as the saying of leaving no stone unturned, leave no thought undisturbed. Expand your definitions and your associations in order to get the best reading from your dreams or visions.

Spine/Spinal Cord

The spine is also a part of the support system. As such, it deals with image, self-confidence, courage and stamina. All thought energy is transmitted through the nerves.

Injuries here denote a doubt in your ability to deal effectively with your current situation. What is going on? Do you feel overwhelmed? Why do you feel that in this situation you can not support yourself?

Squirrels

Squirrels are a part of the rodent family, a possible form of pestilence in material considerations because they climb trees and the tree is symbolic of the material plane.

Is the squirrel trying to get into your reality, into your home; trying to find a place to nest and/or feed? Squirrels also gather and store food for the winter. Is there something that you should be gathering that will help you through the winter months? Is there something that you should be paying attention to? Is there something that you need to be prepared for?

Splinters

First and foremost, splinters are irritants. They are painful and uncomfortable. They can become infected. What is going on that is causing you irritation? What is buried within that can become infected if you do not remove it from your reality?

The symbolic significance also depends on where the splinter gets into the skin because every part of the body has a symbolic interpretation. For a more in-depth study of the body's symbology, refer to my book "Health and Disease Symbology Handbook;" available at www.innerhealthbooks.com.

Stages

Two things come to mind with stages. Go back to "Show or Play" and read that definition. A show or play could be a vehicle of expression.

It could also be the stages of an evolution. From that point of view you could say it is a cycle. You could be looking at something in your dream and watch it go through different stages. Each stage could also be an emotional feeling. Take a look around to see what stage you are in with whatever you are involved in, and see how that relates to you emotionally.

Stars

Stars indicate light within the darkness. Stars provide minor insights. They may be aspects of perception within the doubt. Unless you can study it and understand the properties of the particular star you are looking at, you may not be able to get the insight that is available to you.

Unlike our sun, which lights up the day but can also cause death by sun-stroke, stars simply represent potential insights.

Stepping on something

Whenever you find yourself stepping on something in a dream, it raises a couple of different questions. Are you stepping up or stepping down? What are you stepping on? All sorts of things come to mind, and whatever it is that you are stepping on, from a rock, to a critter, to scat, you need to question and understand what your association is with whatever it is you are stepping on.

Examine what you are stepping on from a symbolic perspective. The act of stepping implies that there is movement. Do you need to take a step? Do you need to step up to something? Do you need to step down from something? Is there something you need to step on? Is there something you need to squash?

Of course, there is always the question of whether or not you feel that you are being stepped on.

Stomach

It is in this sac that you continue the breaking down of your food (thoughts) into a liquid (material life) so it can be assimilated and used as nourishment. Through mental processes you use the things you hear, see and experience. You digest the situations and react according to your concepts.

Difficulties here indicate that the current situations in your life are not easy to digest and accept. Not easy to incorporate into your life.

Stone

A stone is symbolic of defenses. Go back to the Biblical way that the Jews punished people. They would stone them to death.

Jesus said, "… free from sin cast the first stone."[25] The trick there is that if you have no judgments then how can you attack somebody? A stone can also be an offensive weapon; you attack people with an offensive position which is usually a defensive action because you use your defenses to protect yourself.

This action actually walls in your God-Self and prevents that God-Self from communicating, so you are defensive. You also lash out at people through your defenses.

Through the process of reading symbols and applying the information and the control it brings allows you to enter a new level of understanding. This lowering of your defenses allows for the Inner you to manifest.

This accomplishment is noted in Revelations and your new name is written on a white stone.[26] Even so, a stone is not necessarily a defensive measure; stones are also building blocks. The temple was built out of stones.

Store

Stores are basically retail environments. If you work in a store, it could be part of your expression and if you own a store, even more so.

You may feel that stores are places where you can get whatever you need. What kind of a store are you looking at or involved in or inside of in your dream?

From another point of view, stores can provide sustenance and support. They can help you gather the tools you need to do something or give you the strength to persevere through something. What is going on and what kind of a store is it?

Stove

A stove is found in a kitchen, whether commercial or private. Because it is used for cooking, you are dealing with a method of providing sustenance. It can represent expression, as well, especially if you are a cook or baker.

It may also be that you grew up in a time or place where the stove was the fundamental source of heat for the cabin, the house or the room. What is your association with a stove?

Streets

Streets are like highways. They allow you to traverse from point A to point B. Is it a narrow or broad street? Is the street under construction? Is it paved smooth or is it rocky? Does it have holes? What are you trying to traverse? What kind of vehicle are you using on the street? Is the vehicle legal? Do all the lights work?

Streets are certainly tied into your direction and your expression. In what way do streets serve you? In what way do they facilitate your journey? Are you lost? You may be on a street where you cannot decipher the name or it is unfamiliar, or there are no buildings. All different kinds of considerations must be taken.

Sugar

Sugar represents the sweet things in life that promise something and deliver nothing. When you think about sugar from a health perspective, it is a white poison. It is a false promise and a false sense of delight, security and hope.

You can use sugar to mask horrible things. You can make something that is rotten and spoiled taste good with sugar. There are so many thoughts presented to man that are just like sugar. They are empty promises that appear to be good and taste sweet, but they provide no sustenance and no nourishment at all.

In excess, sugar is very detrimental to the body because it can cause diabetes, which can cause nerve death that leads to blindness and amputations and you end up with the inability to have any control over your direction or the handling of your situations.

What is it that you may not want to be looking at? Are you dealing with elevated blood sugar? Are you dealing with diabetes? Do you have all of this wealth around you and yet it provides nothing? Is sugar tied into your expression in some way? Are you a baker or candymaker? Sugar may be an ingredient that is vital to your expression.

Sun/Sunlight

The sun represents inspiration. It provides life and illuminates the dark. It can burn, destroy and blind. There are many different ways to consider the sun and seek to understand what it does.

Sunlight provides insight. Both the sun and sunlight can create shadows and distort the appearance of something. It may be that those symbols are telling you that you need to look at things more closely and bring them into the light so you have a clearer perception.

Sword

This item is definitely symbolic of the "expression of manhood," whether male or female. It is considered so because of its phallic design.

A sword has multiple uses. You can use it to cut through to the "truth" of something. You can use it to defend yourself or to attack another. This is when the "expression of manhood" is used in a defensive mode. See also Vehicles of Expression.

Where was this in your dream and how was it being used? Is there someone or something that you need to defend yourself from? Is there a need to attack and why do you feel that way? Is there something or someone that you need to cut down to size?

T

Tables

Tables are another one of those special elements where your Personal Emotional Association is most important. Tables could represent imposition (if you had to do your homework there), and it is the same with desks. On the other hand, tables and desks could represent creativity, expression.

The kitchen or dining room table could relate to sustenance or family time, as well as an entertaining area because it is where all of the guests and family sit around and talk.

Tack

When I think of a tack, two things come to mind immediately. One, the equipment used for horses and two, a pin. So, a tack, a thumb tack or a pin could all represent the same thing. One would be an irritant, a danger or a discomfort. The other would be used to secure something, such as a notice to a bulletin board.

How many tacks are you seeing and what purpose are they serving? Is there an emotional association? Are they involved somehow in your expression? Did you ever sit on a tack or get stuck with one?

If the dream refers to horse tack, then the questions relate to your involvement with horses. Do you own one? Are you a rider? Do you work in a store that sells tack? How does this type of equipment fit into your life?

In all matters, whenever a symbol comes up it is there because you have an emotional association with it and, more often than not, it relates directly to a very specific event, as opposed to a generalization. See if you can pin down (pun intended) what it is in relationship to.

Tail

A tail can be an extension of an animal, or it could be someone following you, causing you to feel that you were being tailed. If this is the case, what are you involved with that surveillance would be required and by whom?

Again, there needs to be further seeking to understand the type of tail (rabbit, dog, horse, goat, deer, an exceptionally long tail, etc.).

Taste buds

Taste buds are part of your defense system. They detect sweet, sour, pungent, hot, acidic, etc. They are all part of your defense mechanisms because you use your tongue to discern the subtlety of things you are about to consume. In the same way, you should use your eyes and ears to discern the subtlety of the truth of something you are seeing or hearing.

How a tongue appears in your dream or vision depends upon what is currently going on. What do you need to taste? What might be repugnant to your taste? Does something you are working on require more flavor? Or does it require something to increase the taste appeal? Your tongue is also essential for communication.

Your taste buds are there to protect you from swallowing distasteful ideas or toxic concepts that are presented with aromatic or taste enhancements to make them more acceptable or palatable.

ryryry 217

Teacher

Teachers are possessors of knowledge. They set examples by being educators, guides, allies and inspirers. They could also represent authority, suppression, discipline or a personal form of expression. The type of teacher that is displayed is also important because of the meaning of that discipline and the environment. These factors may matter more to you than another setting.

If you are a teacher then the question becomes who was the teacher in the dream? Was it a co-worker and, in that case, what was going on? How do you feel about that person? What do they represent to you?

Teeth

Depending upon which teeth they are, separate interpretations follow. Part of them are tied into communication, part of them are tied into imagery, and part of them are tied into the ability to tear at thoughts and break them down into smaller increments.

Depending upon which tooth it is, it would give you an idea of where there may be a conflict. Either imagery or expression, because it is difficult to enunciate clearly without your front teeth and the lack would create a smile-less expression that would affect your image.

Telephone

Telephones represent communication. You may use a telephone to reach out to people. You may be on the receiving end and you live for phone calls. It may be a cell phone in the dream and not necessarily a desktop phone. Ask yourself how a phone is important to you and how it participates in your expression.

Do you need to reach out and talk to someone? Who were you talking to? What was the nature of the conversation? Did you initiate the call? Did they call you? Why?

Tent

A tent is temporary housing or shelter and a form of protection from the environment. Do you have any particular associations with a tent? Maybe you went camping with your parents, your siblings, your girlfriend, your buddies and something happened that left an emotional association. What happened? How does the tent figure into the rest of the dream?

Do you feel that what you are involved in currently is of a temporary nature? Do you need protection from something for a short period of time? Do you feel that your current level of protection is inadequate?

Termites

Termites eat away at wood, which may or may not be part of your foundation. Either way, they are things that consume, often to the detriment of the structure under attack.

Is there something eating at you? Are you being bothered by little nit-picky things? Is something eating at your foundation/structure? What are the little pests that are distracting you from moving forward?

Testes

The same holds true for the testes that applies to the ovaries. If there are problems here they indicate difficulty with self-image and personal expression.

A man may believe that he cannot express himself, or that he has no authority to bring forth new ideas, or create new things. This would be in keeping with the basic self-image and the expression of manhood.

Throne

The royal throne is the seat of power. Some also refer to the bathroom commode as "the throne." What is your association with a throne?

Were you ever before a royal throne? Do you consider your commode a throne? If so, what does that mean to you? How is it showing up in your dream or vision?

If it is a commode, does it function properly or is it overflowing or stopped up? Does the term "throne" have the power you think it should? Does it manifest it? Do you see yourself in a position of power? Do you want to be in a position of power? Why?

Thunder

Thunder is a loud sound created by natural phenomena, often accompanying lightning. Did you hear thunder in your dream or vision? How do you respond to thunder when you experience it? Does it frighten you? Has it frightened you in the past? Do you enjoy watching thunderstorms? Do you enjoy watching lightning?

Question what thunder means to you. It could be a disturbance or it could stimulate fear or uncertainty. It may be that you have pets that come to you for security and protection when they hear thunder. Look at what else is occurring in the dream and how that works in the entirety.

Thyroid

The thyroid regulates the metabolic rate. It participates in physical and mental growth. It plays a part in your balance between the material and spiritual considerations that you have.

For a greater symbolic understanding of the thyroid and every other gland, organ or system read "Health and Disease Symbology Handbook;" available at www.innerhealthbooks.com.

Ticks

These are small annoyances that eat at you and drain your faith in yourself because they are bloodsuckers, and blood is the spirit of the body. So, they are going to affect your power, your energy, your faith, your spirit, and your inspiration.

What is eating away at you? What or who do you feel is living off of your efforts without reciprocating? In what ways is your faith in yourself being depleted?

Toes

It is a medical fact that without toes, you would have a hard time maintaining your upright position, your balance.

If you are experiencing stubbed toes in your dreams then the questions become: Where were you headed? Why do you think/feel that it could trip you up? Why are you uncertain about this direction?

Toilet

A toilet is used for collecting waste. It is a component of the cleansing apparatus in a home. When it is backed up, much like constipation, there is difficulty in eliminating toxins and waste.

In what ways are you blocked from eliminating waste? In what ways are you hindered from cleansing in the current situation?

Perhaps there is something you are trying to flush down the toilet or there is a feeling that something is being flushed down the toilet. Look around you. What is going on? What do you feel you may be losing control over?

Tongue

The tongue provides the ability to taste the flavors of life and to be able to distinguish which is healthful against which is detrimental. It is also essential to express one's Self.

Read the interpretation of taste buds for there are similarities that will be tied into the symbolic understanding of the tongue.

Torso

Here is where sustenance is digested and distributed to support life. All systems for material life are contained within. The symbolic reflection of some thoughts in conflict manifests here as disease.

The size and shape of your body is also a symbolic reflection of thoughts in action, even when you are not sick or dealing with any kind of condition or ailment.

Train/Plane/Bus

These are all vehicles of expression. As a passenger, you are at the mercy of the driver. You are subject to the subconscious concepts of whoever is in the driver's seat.

A train is limited in where it can go because it is on a track, being confined to a particular direction with no freedom of choice, no way to change direction and make a left, right, or U-turn. There is expression and there is movement, but it is confined and limited in its versatility and ability. See also Vehicles of Expression.

Planes and buses offer more mobility and freedom on one level, yet you are still at the mercy of the driver or pilot's subconscious concepts.

Which vehicle were you riding in your dream? Where were you sitting? What was going on? Where were you going? Did you know the driver? Was that energy familiar? Questions like these will help you come to some insights as to what energies are at work. They may also help you see where you think you are confined and not in control of the forward movement of your own expression.

Trapped

This is easy in the sense that it represents being cornered, confined, and restrained. It may indicate that you are locked into something. You feel imprisoned.

There are all types of traps: rabbit, bear and raccoon traps, to mention but a few. What kind of trap is appearing in your dream and in what way does the structure of the trap reflect other aspects of the dream?

What kind of trap do you feel you are in and do you see a way out? Perhaps your dream is telling you that this is an underlying feeling and with that knowledge it can lead you to make certain decisions that could free you from the trap. However, the reality is that those decisions could, in turn, create a rejection that would have you miss an opportunity or place you in a trap.

What are the things that make you feel trapped and how are those energies currently at work?

Once they and the subconscious concepts that give life to them are understood, then you will be able to free yourself from those energies and concepts that keep you prisoner in your own mind.

Trees

The symbology of the tree is that it represents the material plane. There is a unique aspect, however, since trees take from the material plane, absorbing nutrients from the soil, and give to the spiritual plane by releasing oxygen, spirit, back into the air.

Trees are symbolic of transition and conversion. Tree roots go deep into the earth. They draw their sustenance from the material plane. The nutrients are absorbed out of the soil to feed the tree to a point where a certain chemical mixture reaches the leaves and, through the process of photosynthesis, releases oxygen into the atmosphere.

Tripping on something

Unlike stepping up, tripping means that something could be befuddling you. Where were you going when you tripped? What did you trip on? What is causing you to stumble? What is causing you to be unsure of your footing and your direction? Did tripping cause you to lose balance? Did it knock you off your feet altogether?

In what way was tripping a part of the dream or vision and how does that tie in to what you are currently going through?

U

Uptight

This is symbolic of being uncomfortable in whatever is going on around you. This is outside your norm and your standards of what is acceptable and what you are willing to deal with. When you see this in another person, especially in your dreams, you need to question what that person means to you because everyone in your dream is an aspect of your Self.

Understanding yourself

Understand why you are attracted to the people you are attracted to, why you act the way you do, why you are afraid to act differently, what would be the ramifications, and why you cannot deal with the ramifications.

These are issues that everyone deals with on a daily basis, for the sake of tranquility, for the sake of unity, and for the sake of man-made convention. My wife said to me the other day that you always do the right thing. I think that there are some of us who always do the right thing, even if it is detrimental to the Self. Sometimes we take certain actions, we maintain particular attitudes, and sometimes we deny the Self because it is the right thing to do according to man-made convention.

The only way to break out of these man-made conventions is to understand the God truth, the Universal Truth, and try to live up to that. That is a conflict within itself because in striving to reach that level of understanding and to manifest it in your life means that you may come into conflict with everything that you are about and in conflict with everyone who is a part of your life. And if they are not willing to move in the same direction as you are at the same time, then you have major issues, then you realize that you may not be on the same path anymore.

You may have been in a relationship and a unity that has lasted anywhere from one year to thirty years, and one day you realize that you are on different tracks, have different needs, different desires; your path to enlightenment has taken you one place and the other person's path to enlightenment has taken them somewhere else.

You say, "Well, God speed." Who is right and who is wrong? Is there a right? Is there a wrong? It all comes down to understanding yourself, what your needs are, and seeking to fulfill your needs based on Universal Truth. If you seek to fulfill your needs based on emotions, you are only going to end up in the same place all over again because as long as you try to fulfill your emotions, it is not going to happen.

Underwear

Underwear provides a certain amount of protection and creates a certain image. It depends on whether you are wearing jockey shorts, boxer shorts, thongs, etc. These are all forms of protection of vital areas, so to speak. The question is: Where was the underwear in the vision or dream? What was going on that there is a degree of vulnerability or a feeling of not being protected as thoroughly as one should be?

Underwater

This symbol conveys being submerged, being overwhelmed by the material plane. Remember, water is symbolic of your material life and air is symbolic of your spiritual life. Depending upon what is going on underwater, there is a feeling of being overwhelmed to the point of drowning – in debt, in obligation, in responsibility or the like.

Unicycle

Life requires balance. In order to move forward, you are on your own with no help or support from any external sources, other than your vehicle of expression. See what is going on that requires you to take a more balanced, singular approach so that when the situation presents itself; through understanding; you will be in a position of strength to deal with it and maximize its potential.

Unicorns

On one level, unicorns can be considered in the same manner as horses. Horses are creatures that require discipline before they can be of service to man. Unicorns are mythical creatures that look and function like a horse.

What is going on that requires discipline? What do you need to understand to make something real from something theoretical?

Useless

This is more of a feeling. Symbolically, you could say it is when there is a very strong doubt or fear at work in certain areas of your life. It may also be when the need for rejection is requiring satisfaction, fulfillment.

The rejection comes from creating the energy of uselessness; it will ultimately offend someone, which will create a rejection vibration that will satisfy the need and expectation of that subconscious concept.

Uselessness could also relate to feelings of inadequacy, ineptitude. It could, and would, be based on subconscious concepts taught and reinforced during the formative years.

One has to question what is going on and how you have reacted to this similar situation in the past. By understanding that, you will see where it leads you now and it will give you an opportunity to become useful in altering the outcome of that particular pattern of behavior. In doing so, you no longer resonate to the concept of uselessness, and the more you turn it into useful activity, the more positive the results will be.

Utensil

Utensils are tools to help you do what needs to be done. There are different types of utensils for different applications. You have to look at what type of utensil it is and what the application may be. That, in and of itself, may give you an indication of what realm you need to be paying attention to and where you may need a utensil to help you mold the situation to the outcome you desire.

Umbrella

This device provides protection from the elements, from the sun and the rain. It may help to buffet wind, but could also be upended by wind.

What is going on, and what type of an environment are you in that requires protection? What else was going on in the dream or the experience that would give a clear understanding of where the protection may be required and where an examination of the energies present is necessary?

V

Vehicles of Expression

A vehicle is symbolic of your expression. This interpretation is based on the understanding that your expression is what you use to get you from place to place, just like you use your car to get you from place to place.

Vehicle (parked)

If your car is parked in a dream, then your expression, your mode of expression, your feelings of being able to express are also parked, inactive, and maybe even inoperable.

The vehicle is waiting for you to insert the key, the insight, the understanding to turn it on, to allow the juice to flow, give it life, get the engine cranked, take it out of park and put it in gear.

Life is about moving forward with your vehicle of expression because in life action is everything. That is why discovering insights and understandings is one thing, and talking about them is another thing. However, if you cannot take those insights and understandings and apply them to your life and take a step forward, you will not change your life. One purpose in life is to move, to take action towards your goals.

God loves active participation, not passive acceptance.

If you think about that for your life, it really is a key for living. Have active participation in the flow of life. Put your energies to work. Make it happen. Participate in the continual unfolding of life and Self. This is Heaven.

If you think you are living in Hell, and it certainly appears that way based on man-made things and what man is doing to the environment, then be active in changing it. Do not passively accept what is going on in your life or what is happening around you. Do not tolerate it. Do not accept it. Challenge it and see what happens.

Velvet

Velvet is a luxurious material. What is the material doing in your dream, and is the velvet a particular color? Question the color. Is it red or black velvet? Is it a painting on velvet?

There are other considerations that could tie into giving you a clearer message of the symbology, whether it is cloth or a painting.

Violent

Whenever there is conflict, it is always because of the "expression of manhood." Everyone, male and female, has an expression of manhood. The question about the conflict is: What is going on around you that could lead to a very anger-producing situation?

Before it escalates into physical reality, there needs to be an understanding of what is going on in the immediate. There are tensions brewing and something has the potential to get out of hand and create havoc through a violent response.

Virus

Viruses are interesting because they are not truly living creatures. They only become active inside a host. Viruses attack various aspects of your body and make you sick.

What or who do you feel is attacking you? What is going on that is a potential threat or attack?

Remember that dreams, as well as symbols, are precognitive looks at the energies that are about to unfold. They are letting you know in advance where you are in a cycle, and what is taking form on the horizon in order to validate your current pattern of behavior.

What kind of a virus is looming that could undermine your strength and force you to raise your defenses? What force do you not feel adequately protected against that you cannot prevent such an intrusion? Who might that force be?

Vomiting

Vomiting symbolically takes you right into the concept of rejection. What thoughts have been presented to you that are so uncomfortable, distasteful, abhorrent and indigestible that you have to get them out of your system as quickly as possible, with no thought of digestion or assimilation?

W

Walking

Walking is part of going towards or away from your destination. There are many ways to get to your destination. You can walk, trot, run or crawl. The fact that you are walking indicates a particular speed and comfort level that allows you movement at a particular pace. What are you walking toward or away from?

Wallet

See Purse and Handbag.

Wandering

Wandering can imply uncertainty if you are wandering in unfamiliar terrain. Wandering can also be a seeking if you are wandering in a particular environment, looking for something. Wandering may also be a method of escape or entertainment.

Once again, you need to question your personal association with the entire concept of wandering. Does it elicit feelings of insecurity because your parents wandered all over the country with you in tow? You can begin to see how one must begin to think and search for answers.

Wasps

These represent airborne thoughts and energies that are coming at you that have the potential to cause you discomfort and possibly pain. They are not lofty thoughts, but really mundane and low to the ground; forces that are backing up or that are coming into your life on a mundane level, causing discomfort. They are the kind of energies that you have to deal with.

You cannot just crush them and be done with them. You have to find an alternative plan of action for eliminating them from coming into your reality altogether. Though it may appear to be difficult because you say, "Well, we live in the country," there are certain maneuvers, positions or changes that you can make.

Maybe there is a natural predator, in which case another line of thought would be necessary to come up with a predatory force or a nullifying force to eradicate what it is that you are dealing with.

For every energy that comes into your life, there is another energy that will neutralize it because it is based on the Universal Teaching to turn every disadvantage into its greatest positive potential. But, in order to do that, you have to understand the energy you are dealing with and what is behind it in order to change it.

Look at those aggravating little thoughts. It may be that there are a bunch of little Mickey Mouse things you now have to deal with that are really a pain, yet you have to comply with them so that they are no longer a nuisance. This will allow you to do what you need in order to get what you want, which is comfort in the material because that is the most prevalent energy.

Water

Water is symbolic of your material life. Without water you die within days. Water can also represent fear. If you have ever come close to drowning, water has a particular significance for you.

If you have ever been close to dehydration, that would be another significant aspect. Are you immersed in the water? Are you in over your head?

In representing material considerations, water may indicate that you feel overwhelmed or that you are in a situation in which you may not be able to swim away.

Water also represents sustenance to some degree; not in a nourishing sense, but in a life-preserving sense.

Water into wine

In the Bible, changing water into wine is a symbolic statement of one's ability to turn material endeavors into a sacrament, meaning it becomes of spiritual value and spiritual benefit, and is richer in what it does.

You can see that changing water to wine is a conversion process. If this appears in your dream or vision as a symbol to you, then examine what you need to work on that you have the ability to convert from a material endeavor into something spiritual, into something that would be a sacrament, something that would bring joy and pleasure to many.

Look also to see what attitudes, considerations, policies, standards, values and guides would benefit from conversion.

Weeds

Weeds are interesting in the sense that they can lay dormant. When they do become active they can wreak havoc. At the same time, a weed may look like it is pretty and it will provide for you, like dandelions. This particular weed will provide sustenance through the consumption of its leaves and roots.

It is only through observation and seeking within that you will be able to discern your weeds and know what is weed, what is wheat and what needs to be discarded.

What are the weeds that are at work in your garden? Consider that any undertaking at this point in time is your garden.

How are the weeds manifesting? Can you pull them out without destroying the rest of the garden?

Who or what are the weeds that you need to deal with? What can you do to create a weed free garden?

Wedding

A wedding is a union of two people. It is a contractual agreement to provide for the other person. Everyone thinks of weddings in those terms. However, you could be wedded to your job, your hobby, even your animals in the sense of there being a deep emotional connection.

Question what a wedding means to you on a personal level. You may have attended countless weddings without ever getting married yourself. How does that make you feel? How does that relate to what you are experiencing?

Wheat

Wheat is considered "the staff of life," and also "the bread of life." If you are looking for more sustenance, maybe you need to take what you have and knead it and add other substances to it to make something that is edible and nourishing. Then you can eat it. But if you take wheat the way it is, as a berry, then you have to mill it to make it into flour and mix it with water and yeast and bake it. Then it can provide you with nourishment.

You can have flat bread or, if you add yeast to it, some extra insights, some other additives, you can give life to it, it can rise, it could feed the masses.

So there may be an insight or something you are working on where with a little bit more understanding you may be able to bring something to life that will feed you and others on different levels.

White

White represents the spiritual aspects of any given thing. It could also represent purity and cleanliness.

The white light is a protective barrier that can be used to surround oneself to protect from harm. It could also be used as a laser beam to meta-surgically alter, change, repair, reduce or remove a physical abnormality.

If something is white, look at the symbol and apply the purity and cleanliness attribute.

Another aspect of white is that it lacks color. What is being shown to you? Does it require color to be more pronounced?

Wine

Wine can be a ceremonial beverage or a social beverage. It may be had for entertainment, socializing, religious ceremonies and the like.

If you drink enough of it, it could be used to avoid everything you are going through. You need to understand how and where wine plays a role in your life.

It may be an integral part of your ethnic background or your culture or the way you live. Maybe wine is served at every meal or is a conversation piece or a communication stimulator.

How does wine play an active part of your life? Is it part of your expression? Are you a wine taster or do you earn a living selling wine? Are you a wine steward at a restaurant? Was the wine in a bottle or a glass? Each of those would have symbolic significance.

What is the brand of the wine? Is it a commercial brand or a cheap brand? Was it a $1.49 gallon of wine or a $30 bottle? All of these are relevant and need to be examined in proportion to the rest of the dream.

Wicker

Wicker is a fiber that can be used for many different things. It can be used to make chairs, baskets, hats, etc. How do you relate to the wicker? Is it part of an expression for you? Do you earn a living selling wicker? How does wicker fit into your life and what personal experiences have you had with it? How does that relate to the current dream or vision?

Wolf

The wolf is a predator, a hunter and even a scavenger. When you think of a wolf, you think of a lone hunter. Think outside of the personal emotional association you may have with a dog. A wolf is a solitary hunter looking for opportunities to survive, to succeed.

Also, a wolf may be a force coming at you from within. In what ways could you be ravenous about something that would deplete you? In what do you feel alone, or feel like the lone hunter, where you are the lone provider? How does that relate to what you are going through? Is there a feeling of having to go it alone?

Worms

Worms are a lengthy consideration. You have pin worms, ring worms, earthworms. It depends on what kind of worms, because the ring worm and pin worm may be more parasitic in nature in the sense that they are living off the host, whereas earthworms live within the soil and are essential for converting vegetable matter into soil and nutrients..

Worms can also be used as bait, so see how that relates.

If you are dealing with pin worms, they live in the intestinal tract, as do tapeworms. In both cases, they would be robbing you of nutrients and robbing you of the value of some of the foods you may be eating. The question becomes: What is going on that is parasitic and eating away at your sustenance? Do you feel that there are some who are living off of your efforts? Look at everything going on around you.

Wrists

See Ankles.

X

X-ray equipment

There are three ways of looking at this symbol.

When this shows up in a dream it can represent sustenance, expression or fear. If you ever had a bad experience while being x-rayed or suffered any after effects, then this could indicate an upcoming cycle of discomfort. Look around at what is going on and how that energy is at work.

If you work with the equipment then it would relate to something dealing with expression. Look at where the equipment is positioned. Think about how you interacted with the equipment and the other aspects of the dream. Tie the pieces together. What is going on with your self expression?

If you earn a living in the supply side of the equipment then you need to look at your part and how that might be affected and the affect it will have on you.

Y

Yurt

A shelter/home used by the Mongolian nomads. The symbology is the same as a home; however, it is more akin to a tent. It is a temporary and mobile shelter; protection of a temporary nature.

What is it that you require the kind of protection that you have to take it with you?

Z

Zipper

A zipper is a device that unites two separate things together. Where was the zipper in your dream? Did it work? Was it broken? What are you going through that needs unifying? Are zippers tied into your earning a living?

Epilogue

Every end is a new beginning. You embarked upon the journey of Self enlightenment a long time ago. These additional perspectives can offer a unique focus that manifests as health and peace.

Join me and others of the like mind in working together to participate in changes of Self, society and mankind through Self enlightenment and actualization.

Michael@innerhealthbooks.com

Listen to my live internet radio. For details, visit www.innerhealthbooks.com.

Thank you for your support.

Michael

Endnotes

[1]That belief system is created and shaded by the concepts the person holds as true within their subconscious mind. If you don't know what concepts you are working with in your life you are the "blind being led by the blind", which is yet another Universal Teaching.

[2] Beyond the physical.

[3]The Inner Self knows the truth of everything. Our Inner Self follows a "master" plan, a primary Spiritual directive. That plan is to express the Harmony of the Creative Continuum of God through the understandings and practice of the Universal Principles, Laws expressed in the Teachings. The Outer Self, the Ego, on the other hand, is following another plan. This plan was presented to the child as concepts and patterns. The Ego's plan is based on man-made concepts, programs and teachings.

[4]Exodus 4:37 … visiting the iniquity of the fathers upon the children, and upon the children's children, unto the third and to the fourth generation.

[5]Matthew 12:33 Either make the tree good, and his fruit good; or else make the tree corrupt, and his fruit corrupt: for the tree is known by his fruit.

[6] Cycles are a law of nature. It is an immutable law, a Universal Teaching. If you look about, you can see this teaching in action in nature. The moon circles the Earth, the Earth circles the Sun and the Sun itself is circling a greater Sun in the Universe. Closer to home, you have the seasons of the year which never change their cyclical motions. Spring, Summer, Fall and Winter always follow one another in the same cycles. This demonstrates

the Universal Teaching, "Every end is but a beginning." Though the seasons follow a particular path or sequence, their appearance is changed. Some Summers are hotter than others, some Springs are wetter than others, some Winters are harsher than others. Just as your individual life is influenced by your individual thought patterns, the collective thought patterns of the general populace influence our weather patterns. Cycles have no beginning and no ending, they just flow into each other. There are four cycles, as there are four aspects of the Self, that every human being passes through on a daily, weekly, monthly, and yearly basis. Some cycles take a decade to traverse from point A to point A. The four cycles are named Emotional, Spiritual, Social/Intellectual, Physical/Material. These are all aspects and cycles of the Self.

[7]The term lucid dreaming was coined by Dutch author and psychiatrist Frederik van Eeden in his 1913 article "A Study of Dreams." Proceedings of the Society for Psychical Research

[8]Letter 159 (A.D. 415) To Evodius, My Lord Most Blessed, My Venerable and Beloved Brother and Partner in the Priestly Office, and to the Brethren Who are with Him, Augustine and the Brethren Who are with Him Send Greeting in the Lord.

[9]Your Personal Emotional Association (PEA) with a symbol is the only true interpretation. An example of the Spiritual/Universal interpretation versus the PEA can be seen in the symbolic interpretation of a dog. Dogs are considered to be man's best friend. From this statement you can surmise that dogs represent companionship. However if you have ever been attacked by a dog, then obviously companionship is not an appropriate interpretation for you.

Aggression or fear is a truer interpretation since the dog symbolizes an animal that might attack you again. You see, the most important aspect of the symbol is your Personal Emotional Association with it. Your PEA is the emotional association you attach to an object based on a personal experience.

The mind does not record past experiences or emotions in words; it uses pictures and emotions. The picture that is recorded in your memory may be of a person, place or thing, such as the attacking dog in the example. Those items that are recorded and stored in your subconscious mind are the ones that have left the greatest impression upon you; your impressions are based on emotional experiences.

Each and every emotional experience is associated with an object that was either involved in the experience, or was in some way connected enough for your mind to use it as a springboard for recall. The reason for the recall is because you are a cyclical and pattern-reliant being. Remember, the Universe and everything that is within it flows in cyclic motion.

Symbols are an integral part of Patterns and Cycles. They tell which Pattern is at work and where you are in the Cycle. That is why it is important to seek out your Personal Emotional Association.

You are always in the midst of a pattern of behavior that is seeking to fulfill a subconscious expectation of self. The beauty of life is that by reading symbols you have the opportunity to change the outcome of a particular pattern of behavior. By making an attitude adjustment or a change through understanding and exercising control, you create a different result.

[10]Mark 4:22 For there is nothing hid, which shall not be manifested; neither was any thing kept secret, but that it should come abroad.

[11]Matthew 7:14 Because strait is the gate, and narrow is the way, which leadeth unto life, and few there be that find it.

[12]A vehicle is symbolic of your expression. This interpretation is based on the understanding that your expression is what you use to get you from place to place, just like you use your car to get you from place to place.

[13]Your Personal Emotional Association (PEA) with a symbol is the only true interpretation. An example of the Spiritual/Universal interpretation versus the PEA can be seen in the symbolic interpretation of a dog. Dogs are considered to be man's best friend. From this statement you can surmise that dogs represent companionship. However if you have ever been attacked by a dog, then obviously companionship is not an appropriate interpretation for you. Aggression or fear is a truer interpretation since the dog symbolizes an animal that might attack you again. You see, the most important aspect of the symbol is your Personal Emotional Association with it. Your PEA is the emotional association you attach to an object based on a personal experience.

The mind does not record past experiences or emotions in words; it uses pictures and emotions. The picture that is recorded in your memory may be of a person, place or thing, such as the attacking dog in the example. Those items that are recorded and stored in your subconscious mind are the ones that leave the greatest impression upon you; your impressions are based on emotional experiences.

Each and every emotional experience is associated with an object that was either involved in the experience, or was in some way connected enough for your mind to use it as a springboard for recall.

The reason for the recall is because you are a cyclical and pattern-oriented being. Remember, the Universe and everything that is within it flows in cyclical motion. Symbols are an integral part of Patterns and Cycles. They tell which Pattern is at work and where you are in the Cycle. That is why it is important to seek out your Personal Emotional Association.

You are always in the midst of a pattern of behavior that is seeking to fulfill a subconscious expectation of self. The beauty of life is that by reading symbols you have the opportunity to change the outcome of a particular pattern of behavior. By making an attitude adjustment or a change through understanding and exercising control, you create a different result.

[14]Matthew 7: 13-14 Enter ye in at the strait gate: for wide is the gate, and broad is the way, that leadeth to destruction, and many there be which go in thereat: Because strait is the gate, and narrow is the way, which leadeth unto life, and few there be that find it.

[15]Matthew 13:16 But blessed are your eyes, for they see: and your ears, for they hear.

[16] Deuteronomy 12:23 Only be sure that thou eat not the blood: for the blood is the life; and thou mayest not eat the life with the flesh.

[17]Matthew 18:3. And said, Verily I say unto you, except ye be converted, and become as little children, ye shall not enter into the kingdom of heaven.

[18]Deuteronomy 12:15-16 Notwithstanding thou mayest kill and eat flesh in all thy gates, whatsoever thy soul lusteth after, according to the blessing of the Lord thy God which he hath given thee: the unclean and the clean may eat thereof, as of the roebuck, and as of the hart. Only ye shall not eat the blood; ye shall pour it upon the earth as water.

[19]Deuteronomy 14:10. And whatsoever hath not fins and scales ye may not eat; it is unclean unto you.

[20]Genesis 1:27. So God created man in his own image, in the image of God created he him; male and female created he them.

[21]Genesis 1:5 And God called the light Day, and the darkness he called Night. And the evening and the morning were the first day.

[22] Jesus said, "If they say to you, 'From where have you originated?,' say to them, 'We have come from the Light, where the Light has originated through itself. It [stood] and it revealed itself in their image.' If they say to you, 'Who are you?' say, 'We are His sons and we are the elect of the Living Father .' If they ask you, 'What is the sign of your Father in you?,' say to them, 'It is a movement and a rest.'"

23 This is a very common pattern. For example, a person starts on a path (job, relationship, etc.). They work their way up the ladder to success or completion in a short period of time. Somewhere along their path to success (or completion), an energy will be injected. This energy could be in the form of someone offering a different opportunity; it may be a statement that offends someone or some kind of circumstance that will create a problem. Some energy of a negative feeling or thought will manifest in that person's life. This feeling becomes the justification for not going any further on the path to success or completion. Without understanding and controlling your Belief System, problems are destined to arise in your life. Without this understanding, you are at the mercy of your Patterns of Behavior. This pattern works this way every time.

24 Genesis 1:27 So God created man in his own image, in the image of God created he him; male and female created he them.

25 John 8:7 …He that is without sin among you, let him first cast a stone at her.

26Revelation 2:17. He that hath an ear, let him hear what the Spirit saith unto the churches; To him that overcometh will I give to eat of the hidden manna, and will give him a white stone, and in the stone a new name written, which no man knoweth saving he that receiveth it.